Changing
School Reading Programs
Principles and Case Studies

S. Jay Samuels
University of Minnesota

P. David Pearson
University of Illinois at Urbana-Champaign

Editors

ira

Published by the
International Reading Association
Newark, Delaware 19714

INTERNATIONAL READING ASSOCIATION

Copyright 1988 by the
International Reading Association, Inc.

Library of Congress Cataloging-in-Publication Data

Changing school reading programs–Principles and Case
Studies.

   Bibliography: p.
   1. Reading (Elementary) – United States. 2. Educational inno-
vations – United States. I. Samuels, S. Jay. II. Pearson, P.
David.
LB1573.C4385   1988   372.4   87-22532
ISBN 0-87207-790-X

Contents

Foreword

T he call for reform in the public schools *(A Nation at Risk)*, in teacher education *(Carnegie Report, Holmes Group Report)*, in higher education *(The Closing of the American Mind)*, and in the teaching of reading *(Becoming a Nation of Readers)* indicates considerable unease with all levels of education in the United States.

Calls for national educational reform or other major social redress historically have advocated extreme and simplistic remedies. Thus, the nostrum advocated for public school reform is an emphasis on the teaching of basic skills. The panacea suggested for a redirection of teacher education is an increase in liberal arts requirements. The solution recommended for the revitalization of higher education is the study and synthesis of the great books. The remedies prescribed for improving the teaching of reading in the schools are a stronger focus on the reading/writing connection and an emphatic shift to the teaching of comprehension as a first priority.

Much as we might take comfort in the assumption that these calls for major educational reform are irrevocably and successfully linked to the proposed solutions, the realities of social, cultural, and educational improvements are more closely related to individual accomplishments than to national movements.

It was the accomplishments of Martin Luther King that defined the noble goals of passive resistance to racial segregation. It was the stubborn will of Eleanor Roosevelt that kept alive the liberal conscience of the American people before, during, and after World War II. And so it is with all significant and lasting change.

Changing School Reading Programs: Principles and Case Studies serves three major purposes.

First, the broadly stated principles for reading program

change provide reasonable curriculum guidelines and common sense instructional expectations for improving reading in the schools. Second (and to my view more important), the text documents when, how, and why individual teachers, separate schools, and independent school districts have implemented highly favorable reading curriculum/practice changes. Third, the text provides teachers, faculty, and schools with the initial impetus for overcoming three persistent obstacles to educational change: inertia, fear, and tradition.

I have never believed in the effectiveness of nationally directed educational or social movements in a democratic society; indeed, I am suspicious of most of them. My education heroes always have been real people; my school heroines have been very much a part of the human society.

Teachers will be better when individual teachers decide they *will* be better, faculties will be better when the collective faculty decides it *will* be better, and schools will be better when the schools themselves decide they *will* be better. I trust this text will help to provide some intelligent directions in the search for better schools. Ideally, it also will help to initiate and sustain the intellectual courage to help all of us reach those decisions.

John C. Manning
University of Minnesota

Prologue

A t the International Reading Association's 1983 convention, I
was on my way to a preconvention institute David Pearson and
I had organized on building exemplary reading programs and initiating changes when a newspaper headline caught my eye: "Presidential Commission on Excellence in Education Finds Faults with Schools." Were the Commission report and the institute on change unrelated events, or did common factors underlie both? I prefer to believe they are related. I believe the underlying factors are that American public schools are essential to the welfare of our society and that schools could be doing a better job. How can schools bring about the needed changes?

Introducing change in a major institution is always difficult. Important institutions require stability; unfortunately, inflexibility and resistance to change tend to go along with stability. To exacerbate the situation, individuals who work in institutions also resist change. They are used to certain patterns of behavior, and changing these patterns can be upsetting.

To overcome institutional inertia and bring about desired changes in our schools, we need theories about how to change institutions and examples of how changes have been achieved. Fortunately, the necessary ingredients are available for improving the quality of reading programs in our schools. This book contains theories and examples school personnel need to bring about change. Included are updated adaptations of the original papers given at the preconvention institute, as well as additional commissioned papers. While the focus of this volume is on how to introduce change in reading programs, readers should note that no particular approach to reading (such as a meaning approach or a skills emphasis) is advocated. Also, with minor modifications, the theories and methods outlined should work for a variety of subject areas in addition to reading.

School personnel should realize that the task of bringing about change is so complex that a single book cannot present every issue on the topic. Yet we believe this book is sufficiently complete that it can be used by school personnel as a blueprint for improving the quality of reading instruction.

SJS

Contributors

Thomas W. Bean
California State University
Fullerton, California

Robert Calfee
Stanford University
Stanford, California

Douglas Carnine
University of Oregon
Eugene, Oregon

Avon Crismore
Purdue University
Fort Wayne, Indiana

Jean Funderburg
Stanford University
Stanford, California

Margaret C. Gallagher
City University of New York
Flushing, New York

Irene W. Gaskins
Benchmark School
Media, Pennsylvania

Anne Goudvis
University of Illinois
Champaign, Illinois

Ramona Newton Hao
Kamehameha Schools
Honolulu, Hawaii

Marcia Henry
Stanford University
Stanford, California

Linda Meyer
University of Illinois
Champaign, Illinois

P. David Pearson
University of Illinois
Champaign, Illinois

S. Jay Samuels
University of Minnesota
Minneapolis, Minnesota

Carol M. Santa
School District #5
Kalispell, Montana

Harry Singer
University of California
Riverside, California

Robert J. Tierney
Ohio State University
Columbus, Ohio

David L. Tucker
Illinois State University
Normal, Illinois

Part one
Basic principles

Prelude

J ay Samuels is probably best known for his work on the development of reading theory and the concept of automaticity. For over a decade, Samuels has been a student of the "effective schools" literature. He has been especially interested in studies of schools in which "at risk" students have achieved at levels far exceeding their demographically similar counterparts and the expectations our society and our educational system typically hold for them. In this chapter, Samuels gives us a broad view of this literature, providing a set of principles that consistently characterize schools that succeed beyond expectation. This chapter should be read as an overview for the remainder of the book, particularly the case studies in Part Two. In reading parlance, Samuels' chapter contains many main ideas; the details will come later.

1

S. Jay Samuels

Characteristics of exemplary reading programs

R ecent evaluations of public education in the United States have been highly critical and have called for change in educational programs. Since change is inevitable, the problem facing our schools is one of producing change in desired directions fast enough to meet a variety of challenges.

One challenge is to improve the quality of reading programs so all students will become literate. This chapter describes the context and characteristics of outstanding reading programs in the hope that our current understanding of what is outstanding will influence our future goals.

An outstanding reading program is considerably more than a reading method; a reading program has numerous connecting parts. Components include assumptions about children's ability to learn and about the role of schools, school personnel, teacher training and supervision, and curriculum. I will discuss these components, followed by a brief section on differences between schools at upper and lower socioeconomic levels.

Underlying assumptions

Where exemplary reading programs are found, administrators and teachers share certain assumptions regarding the role of schools and student potential. The first assumption is that the school is the key factor in student success and failure. By having a good program, the school can have a significant impact on the academic achievement of its students. Consequently, the school holds itself responsible to a large extent for both the successes and failures of its students (Edmonds, 1982).

The second assumption shared by administrators and teachers is that virtually all students can master the basics of literacy. When a student is failing academically, the staff does not absolve the school of responsibility with excuses such as "poor motivation," "lack of readiness," or "poor home background." Instead, teachers in academically successful schools believe teaching includes problem analysis and decision making. Through consistent evaluation of student progress, teachers seek ways to help each student master reading skills (Samuels, 1982).

Significant improvements in a school district may take from three to six years. Consequently, school district leaders must make a long term commitment to academic improvement. Since improving schools usually involves changing teacher attitudes and beliefs, as well as the methods used to instruct students, school leaders must allocate time for regular staff meetings for assessing needs and for planning, implementing, and evaluating educational changes (Berman & McLaughlin, 1978).

To promote teacher cooperation, program goals and the means for their implementation must be developed cooperatively by administrators and teachers. When goals and methods requiring significant teacher investment of time and energy come from the central office staff without shared input from teachers, the district can expect teachers to resist program implementation. When teachers and administrators work together to establish goals and methods, schools are successful in instituting planned change. They attempt to develop staff consensus regarding goals and the means of achieving them. Teachers in such schools direct instructional effort at these clearly defined instructional goals. Implementation is checked regularly and carefully, and evaluation results are shared. Teachers are encouraged to work together to achieve the program goals (Berman & McLaughlin, 1978; Lipham, 1980).

Successful schools provide a context for good instruction by protecting classroom time from disruption and by establishing routines that ensure safe and orderly school buildings and classrooms. Administrators and teachers must communicate to students that high standards of behavior are required in order for academic goals to be achieved. School building and classroom behavior standards and consequences are established in advance. The standards can be developed by students in conjunction with school staff. However, the number of rules should be kept to a minimum; too many rules are difficult to enforce and may encourage students to test every rule to find out which ones will be enforced. Rules should be written, reviewed regularly, and enforced consistently (Brophy, 1979; Kounin, 1977; Weber, 1971).

Personnel

Administrators

Individual teachers working alone can raise the level of achievement in their own classrooms, but strong administrative leadership is essential to bring about school and districtwide change and improvement. The administrative leader provides encouragement, creates an organizational climate that fosters cooperative planning and program implementation, provides time for faculty planning, secures necessary financial support, and opposes foes of long range school change and improvement (Becker, 1977; Berman & McLaughlin, 1978; Weber, 1971).

Teachers

Teachers' beliefs are critical to the success of the program. Teachers in exemplary programs believe they are capable of helping each student master the essentials of reading, that student failure is not acceptable, and that student success and failure depend largely on what happens in the classroom (Edmonds, 1982; Harris & Serwer, 1966).

Teachers are more likely to support ambitious, demanding programs they have helped to develop than routine projects. Teachers are willing to take on the extra work of program improvement if they believe their efforts will make them better teachers and help their students (Samuels & Edwall, 1976).

Other personnel

A number of successful reading programs use reading specialists who serve as teacher trainers or on the job consultants or provide materials for classrooms (Becker, 1977; Weber, 1971; Wilder, 1977). Exemplary programs often use paraprofessional aides for direct instruction after they have been trained by the classroom teacher or a reading specialist (Becker, 1977; Hawkridge, Tallmadge, & Larsen, 1968). Some successful programs use parents as part of the instructional team. Functions performed by parent volunteers range from helping students in the classroom to helping their own children at home. When parents are used in a program, teachers provide them with specific guidelines and techniques for helping children (Levine, 1982, Wilson, 1981).

Teacher training and supervision

Successful programs inevitably provide teachers with additional training through inservice education. Effective inservice training has a number of characteristics:

- Concrete, teacher specific, and ongoing
- Classroom assistance from project staff
- Observation of excellent teaching in other classrooms
- Regular project meetings
- Teacher participation in project decisions
- Principal participation in training

Once goals and methods are agreed on by the staff, implementation is checked regularly. Evaluation is ongoing, and program successes and shortcomings are noted. When goals are not met, the staff meets to plan new approaches (Samuels, 1982).

Curriculum

Successful programs are characterized by changes in the school reading curriculum. Aspects of school reading programs that appear to be related to successful programs include duration of project, teaching word recognition skills, objectives, time on task, structure, lecture orientation, and assessment practices.

Duration of project

Often, government and school officials are overly optimistic about the amount of time needed to produce stable improvements in school programs. Successful change often takes six years. Studies of school change indicate the first two years are needed to do needs assessements, establish priorities, alter staff beliefs and attitudes, and improve instruction. The next two years are needed to implement the plan, with an additional two years needed to produce a stable effect (Berman & McLaughlin, 1978).

Word recognition skills

In successful programs, skilled word recognition is considered a prerequisite for good comprehension. Most successful programs include instruction in phonics and other word recognition skills. In addition, they provide experience in reading meaningful and interesting material in context (Weber, 1971; Wilder, 1977).

Objectives

In general, successful reading programs have clear, specific objectives, and these are displayed publicly so staff, students, and community know the goals. The materials and methods used in the programs are appropriate for the objectives (Cohen, 1981; Weber, 1971).

Time on task

While it is important to allocate enough time for learning to take place, it is also important to organize the class so time is used effectively. In successful programs, teachers have organized the class so they can devote as much time as possible to goal related instructional activities (Rosenshine, 1976; Wilder, 1977).

Structure

In successful programs, the teacher does not have to spend instructional time organizing and directing regular activities. Successful classrooms are described as orderly rooms where little time is wasted on discipline, on giving instructions, or on moving from one activity to another (Becker, 1977; Rosenshine, 1976). Many routine activities are handled by students, using a system in which the teacher models an activity and then gradually allows students to assume responsibility for it (Singer & Donlan, 1985).

Lecture orientation

For each lesson, students are told what the goals are, how the lesson fits in with previous work, and why the work is important. To check understanding of an assignment, the teacher asks pertinent questions and gives students an opportunity to respond (Levin, 1981).

Assessment practices

There is frequent informal and formal monitoring of student progress in exemplary programs. The information is used to make diagnostic decisions about individual students and to evaluate the overall progress of the reading program (Becker, 1977; Hawkridge, Tallmadge, & Larson, 1968).

Differences between high and low socioeconomic schools

The characteristics of effective school programs described so far hold true regardless of the socioeconomic level of the school. However, the most recent studies of effective schools indicate there are some subtle differences between upper and lower socioeconomic schools. In low socioeconomic schools, the emphasis is on basic skills, homework expectations are moderate, instructional leaders exert high levels of control over instruction, home-school links tend to be moderate to weak, and rewards given to students are extrinsic and frequent. In high socioeconomic schools, curricular emphasis extends beyond basic skills, homework expectations are high, instructional leaders exert moderate control over instruction, home-school links are strong, and rewards are more intrinsic and less frequent (Hallinger & Murphy, 1986).

Conclusion

As this description of exemplary reading programs suggests, there is considerably more to an excellent reading program than a method; numerous components of the curriculum must receive attention if the goal of universal literacy is to be achieved. Although building an excellent reading program is difficult and time consuming, the goal is so important that it is worth the effort. How this goal can be achieved is discussed in the following chapters.

References

Becker, W.C. Teaching reading and language to the disadvantaged: What have we learned from field research? *Harvard Educational Review,* 1977, *47,* 518-543.

Berman, P., and McLaughlin, M.W. Federal programs supporting educational change. Volume 8, *Implementing and sustaining innovations.* Santa Monica, CA: Rand Corporation, 1978.

Brophy, J. Teacher behavior and its effects. *Journal of Educational Psychology,* 1979, *71,* 733-750.

Cohen, M. Effective schools: What the research says. *Today's Education,* April-May 1981, 46-48.

Edmonds, R.R. Programs of school improvement: An overview. *Educational Leadership,* 1982, *40* (3), 4-11.

Hallinger, P., and Murphy, J.F. The social context of effective schools. *American Journal of Education,* 1986, *94,* 328-355.

Harris, A., and Serwer, B. The CRAFT Project: Instructional time in reading research. *Reading Research Quarterly,* 1966, *1* (2), 27-57.

Hawkridge, D.G., Tallmadge, G.K., and Larsen, D.R. *A study of selected exemplary programs for the education of disadvantaged children.* Final Report, volume 1. (ED 023 776)

Kounin, J.S. *Discipline and group management in classrooms.* Huntington, NY: Robert Kreiger Publishing, 1977.

Levin, T. *Effective instruction.* Alexandria, VA: Association for Supervision and Curriculum Development, 1981.

Levine, D. Successful approaches for improving academic achievement in inner-city elementary schools. *Phi Delta Kappan,* 1980, *63* (8), 523-526.

Lipham, J.A. Change agentry and school improvements: The principal's role. *Interorganizational arrangements for collaborative efforts.* Portland, OR: Northwest Regional Educational Laboratory, 1980.

Rosenshine, B. Recent research on training behaviors and student achievement. *Journal of Teacher Education,* 1976, *27,* 61-65.

Samuels, S.J. Characteristics of successful school programs in basic skills. In Spencer Ward and Linda Reed (Eds.), *Basic skills: Issues and choices.* Washington, DC: National Institute of Education, 1982.

Samuels, S.J., and Edwall, G. An overview of the research literature on educational innovation. In J.T. Guthrie (Ed.), *A study of the locus and nature of reading problems in elementary schools.* Washington, DC: National Institute of Education, 1976.

Weber, G. *Inner-city children can be taught to read: Four successful schools.* Washington, DC: Council for Basic Education, 1971.

Wilder, G. Five exemplary reading programs. In J.T. Guthrie (Ed.), *Cognition, curriculum, and comprehension.* Newark, DE: International Reading Association, 1977.

Wilson, R.G. The effects of district-wide variables on student achievement. In K.A. Keithwood and A. Hughes (Eds.), *Curriculum Canada III.* Vancouver, BC: University of British Columbia, 1981, 73-88.

Prelude

C hapter 2, a mammoth effort by Margaret
   Gallagher, Anne Goudvis, and David Pearson,
is the most conventionally academic chapter in this
book. Along with Carnine's Chapter 4, it is also the
densest in terms of the number of novel concepts presented. However, a modestly paced journey through
this history and current events treatment of the research on the process of social change is well worth
your effort. The authors begin with research on the
change process in industrial, agricultural, and social
settings, the arenas in which social change has been
studied for over half a century. After introducing basic principles of change, they discuss the crucial issue
of knowledge transfer before plunging into the
"change in education" literature. They lay the ground-
work for the directed development and mutual adaptation models so crucial to Meyer's analysis in Chapter
3. The authors conclude that, while there is no one
best general model of change that will always work,
each circumstance has some special optimal combination of change processes. This chapter deserves two
readings — one for a quick overview and one for more
careful digestion. The chapter provides readers with a
useful framework for studying and classifying the
programs and methods reported in the chapters that
follow it.

Margaret C. Gallagher
Anne Goudvis
P. David Pearson

2

Principles of organizational change

T he study of how changes and innovations replace or modify existing views and practices is relatively young in the field of education, and even younger in the field of reading. However, there is a longstanding tradition of serious study of change in the fields of sociology, political science, and industrial psychology. To provide a general context for other chapters in this volume, we have outlined a framework with three major divisions: (1) we describe and consider some general strategies for change as well as a series of issues generally associated with change; (2) we consider specific change in education, distinguishing between change at the organizational level and change at the teacher or classroom level; and (3) we offer some conclusions about change in educational programs and some advice to those who have the goal of changing school reading programs.

Strategies for change

Change scholars have identified generic strategies used to induce change. The most general classification has been developed by Chin and Benne (1969), although several other authors have developed classifications as well (Morrish, 1976; Zaltman & Duncan, 1977; Zaltman, Florio, & Sikorski, 1977). Chin and Benne identify three basic strategies: empirical rational, normative reeducative, and power coercive.

Empirical rational strategies

These strategies reflect the hope of science as the savior of society. Two basic assumptions underlie their use: (1) people are rational beings, and (2) rational self-interest will spur people toward change when they perceive it to be desirable. Chin and Benne trace the roots of commitment to an empirical rational approach in America and Western Europe to the Age of Enlightenment and classic liberalism, a period in which scientific investigation and education were believed to play the principal roles in dispelling ignorance and advancing the human state. Chin and Benne suggest six basic sub-strategies (annotated in parentheses) that have prevailed through general social adherence to an empirical rational approach:

1. Basic research and dissemination of knowledge through education (know the truth and the truth will make you free).
2. Personnel selection and replacement policies (get the most dynamic person for the job).
3. Systems analysts as staff consultants (get help when breakdowns occur).
4. Applied research and diffusion systems for dissemination of research results (translate basic science into technology and spread the word).
5. Utopian thinking (encourage people to think grand thoughts).
6. Perceptual and conceptual reorganization through clarification of language (make sure everyone "talks the same language").

Normative reeducative strategies

The assumptions underlying normative reeducative strategies (which are really strategies that promote problem solving) are fundamentally different from those that emanate from an empirical rational approach. Chin and Benne trace commitment to a normative reeducative approach to the influence of Dewey (1967) and Lewin (1951) and their intellectual descendants (Bennis, Benne, & Chin, 1969; Bradford, Benne, & Gibb, 1964; Lippit, 1969). A third influential force was Freud's development (1972) of the client/therapist relationship as a tool for changing the client. Dewey's influence stems from his belief in the transactional nature of the relationship between people and the environment and Dewey's development of the concept of social intelligence at work to humanize the scientific method. Lewin's influence can be traced to his development of collaborative relationships among researchers, educators, and activists to integrate the processes of research, training, and action in the solution of human problems.

Commitment to a normative reeducative approach to change has given rise to two basic substrategies: problem solving and professional development. A problem solving orientation stresses collaborative efforts to identify problems, organize plans for appropriate data collection, search for potential solutions, and evaluate trial solutions. The staff development orientation focuses on fostering the growth potential of individuals as a force in organizational change. Both orientations depend on climates characterized by openness and trust among members within groups as well as between groups. In short, these strategies emphasize personal growth and a cooperative spirit.

Power coercive strategies

These strategies emphasize the use of economic, political, or moral sanctions in the exercise of power. Chin and Benne describe three substrategies within the power coercive approach: nonviolence, political pressure, and recomposition and manipulation of power elites. Sit ins, demonstrations, and boycotts are examples of nonviolent approaches. Lobbying by special interest groups in order to influence state and federal legislation affecting educational policies demonstrates the use of political pressure. Poverty program designs, which have included participation by client populations, may be viewed as attempts to redress basic power imbalances.

In education, teacher strikes and legislative mandates represent the most common uses of power coercive strategies.

Persuasion strategies

Chin and Benne (1969) do not include persuasion as a change strategy; however, Zaltman and Duncan (1977) do. Because we believe persuasion to be such a pervasive strategy for change within education, we include it here. Persuasion is not usually used as a single strategy; it tends to be used in conjunction with the other strategies. Persuasion is characterized by the use of charismatic and other personal factors to convince individuals and organizations to change.

Our separate discussion of each strategy may give the false impression they are mutually exclusive. To the contrary, most change efforts use combinations of all of them. Nonetheless, even the most eclectic of change efforts tends to focus on one of these strategies.

Although we have used technical and opaque language to describe these change strategies, we see them in use on almost a daily basis. All change efforts involve someone who promotes the change, i.e., a change agent. There is a convenient analogy between change agent strategies and sales promotion. Using a rational empirical strategy, the change agent sends information into the free marketplace of ideas, hoping someone will see fit to purchase it. The agent operates much like a company that relies on direct mail advertising: both must wait for consumers to take the bait. Adopting a persuasive strategy, the change agent operates like a traveling salesperson who tries to drum up business through personal techniques as well as through the quality of the product. With a normative reeducative strategy, a change agent is like a stockbroker or home decorator: the agent offers advice in response to a client initiated need, and ultimately a product or service is negotiated in a transactive mode. The analogy also holds for the coercive strategy; here the agent for change might be likened to a lobbyist who uses veiled threats or promises of support to get a position adopted via legislative or executive mandate.

Issues in knowledge production and utilization

Whether large or small in scope, change involves some attendant issues that concern the production, availability, and use of knowledge; motivation for change; and questions of interpersonal relations. Often there are technical questions concerning either the implementation of change effort or dissemination of results. Because they are implicated in every effort to implement change, we discuss each of these issues at length.

In the process of intentional efforts toward change, knowledge — whether newly created or newly available — typically precipitates or supports change. While the dissemination of knowledge is a key element in rational empirical strategies, it is usually at least a part of other strategies, especially normative reeducative ones. Again, there is a long history of research on knowledge use, most of it coming from fields like industrial psychology and agriculture.

How knowledge is used

Knowledge utilization chains have been used to characterize the flow of information in change models (Havelock & Havelock, 1973). The simplest chain represents a one way flow from knowledge producer (researcher) to linking agent or practitioner (teacher, doctor, county agent) to consumer (student, patient, farmer). Obviously, authoritarian models of change use such a chain, but so do other approaches, including those that emphasize empirical rational strategies.

A slightly more complex model allows for two way flow of information and includes the flow from consumer to producer. Feedback allows for at least some modification of the questions that basic and applied researchers deal with by those who are supposed to use the knowledge researchers generate. A normative reeducative strategy of change will encourage this two way flow of information, because the strategy demands feedback from the linking agents or consumers of knowledge.

Both these models are too simplistic to account for what really happens as knowledge goes from being generated to being used. While the metaphor of a chain suggests that knowledge moves smoothly from producer to consumer, there are many barriers to information flow. The chain metaphor fails to consider complex issues that arise among people who are the producers, linking agents, and consumers of knowledge. Havelock and Benne (1969) developed a more complete picture of how knowledge gets used by considering three factors: motivational issues (Do people want this knowledge?), interpersonal and group membership issues (How do personal values and social status help or hinder knowledge flow?), and technical issues (Is the medium the message?). These factors help to explain what motivates knowledge use in the first place and how and why some knowledge gets used faster and more widely than other knowledge.

Motivational issues. Scientists or other knowledge producers run the risk of producing knowledge no one wants. Knowledge can have little or no cash value; if no one is interested in a particular piece of knowledge, there is no motivation for anyone to put it to use.

The psychological, as opposed to the real, urgency of a problem or need to which knowledge applies also influences how widely knowledge may be understood and supported. For example, work on polio (a crippling but not fatal disease) received tremendous and immediate public support, while work on lung cancer (more likely to be fatal but less disfiguring) has gone unheeded by many.

Interpersonal and group membership issues. Many barriers to information flow arise because information must pass from members of one group to those of another. Some groups are more insular (isolated from outside influences), while others are more permeable (receptive to outside influences). Scientists working on a top secret defense project form an insular, impermeable group, whereas a group of teachers working to select a new social studies text for their district are a more permeable group, subject to the influence of others. In particular, issues concerning group members' status and values account for permeability (or the lack of it) between groups.

In general, the higher the status of individuals, the greater the likelihood that they will gain the ear of another group. High status tends to be positively correlated with age (both the very young and the very old have low status), education, specialization, and the social status of the discipline within which one works (e.g., medicine > education). Status comes into play when one considers how the work of a basic researcher is brought to the attention of a consumer.

Gallagher, Goudvis, Pearson

The people who do the linking (the dissemination and development people) often suffer from social status problems (Havelock & Benne, 1969) and are unsure about their place in the entire system. For instance, a curriculum coordinator is likely to possess neither the status of the university professor nor the credibility of the classroom teacher.

Status is also important in another dimension. In getting a group to change, there are two kinds of key people who need to be co-opted: the opinion leaders in the group and, ironically, the potential troublemakers who, though low in status, might oppose the opinion leaders in their attempts to adopt the change.

Value orientation is a critical problem in getting practitioners to use knowledge produced by the researchers. Knowledge builders tend to want to produce knowledge that is general, unitary, and futuristic. They want to build knowledge that is broadly applicable across many contexts and are willing to *wait* for research to yield accurate information before they worry about application. Practitioners want knowledge that is unique, pluralistic, and immediate. They are concerned with specific clients, they expect that knowledge will not apply uniformly across contexts, and they want the knowledge *now,* however imperfect it may be. Value differences of this magnitude can lead to mistrust and misunderstanding of motives between people in these groups, thus reducing the likelihood that new knowledge will be incorporated into practice.

Technical issues. Translating the technical ideas of knowledge producers into understandable language for consumers has always been a difficult job for those seeking to be knowledge brokers. As knowledge is transmitted, its potential impact can be increased or decreased as a function of the technical quality of the information itself and the manner of transmission. Recoding appears to be the critical step in preparation. Not only must the ideas be made understandable to the user, but their potential value must be highlighted. As in the production of consumer goods, packaging and labeling help to determine the extent of use. With respect to transmission, the medium is all important. One recent study of the National Diffusion Network (Emrick, Peterson, & Agarwala-Rogers, 1977) has suggested the importance of personal contact between the linkage agent and the practitioner (apparently they feel it is not enough just to send the truth out into the world).

The implication of these issues in knowledge use seems rather straightforward. In order to promote the use of new knowledge, something more than publishing a set of technical documents written for our colleagues is necessary. What is required is a much more context sensitive orientation to knowledge utilization, an orientation in which we concern ourselves with conscious attempts to build channels of communication that take into account the needs and motives of the consumer, the values of all concerned parties, and the effectiveness of various modes of dissemination.

Change in education

We turn now from a look at the broad issues in social and technological change to a narrower focus on attempts to produce changes in school practices. We examine this literature from three perspectives: (1) We look at some historical evidence evaluating the degree to which the four change strategies discussed at the outset of this chapter have operated in education; (2) we look at the evaluations of large scale change efforts, attempts to make an educational institution shift its focus rather dramatically; and (3) we examine the literature on professional development and teacher change.

A historical perspective on change in education

The empirical rational strategy of change has not always worked well in education, especially when people have tried to impose large scale changes on small organizational units (Berman & McLaughlin, 1975). However, it can be used to explain relatively small scale changes on large organizational units (i.e., a nation or a state).

Three examples are particularly noteworthy. First, Clifford (1978) has offered a particularly thoughtful and well documented account of the impact that E.L. Thorndike's work in vocabulary and word frequency in the 1920s had on vocabulary control in children's reading books and content area texts published in the 1930s, 1940s, and 1950s. It represents a classic example of a linking process from

Gallagher, Goudvis, Pearson

basic research (Thorndike) to applied researchers (such as Gates, Bond, Russell, and Gray) to publishers (many of the applied researchers also authored basal series) to local school districts.

Second, while it remains for historians to document the exact reasons for the widescale incorporation of phonics instruction into basal reading programs in the early 1970s, it is likely they will notice the correlative timeliness of the publication of Chall's *Learning to Read: The Great Debate* (1967) along with Bond & Dykstra's research program in first grade reading instruction (1967). Chall came out in favor of more code emphasis earlier in reading programs and, when all the guarded disclaimers are set aside, so did Bond and Dykstra. While some might argue that Chall's influence illustrates a persuasive rather than a rational empirical strategy of change (and they might disagree with the objectivity of her research synthesis), the flow of information use has all the characteristics typical of the empirical rational strategy.

A third example is just now coming to fruition. In 1961, Robert McNamara transported the management by objectives movement from industry into the U.S. Defense Department. In the middle and late 1960s, educational psychologists such as Bloom (1968), Gagne (1967, 1970), Glaser (1967), Mager (1962), and Popham et al. (1969) began constructing models of instruction based on mastery learning models. An important component of these models has been the clear specification of behavioral objectives that pinpoint precisely those behaviors students are supposed to engage in to demonstrate competence on a variety of subcomponents of the process or knowledge domain to be learned. Gradually, this movement gathered impetus and spread to a variety of governmental and educational efforts. For example, the entire Right to Read effort initiated in 1970 used the prevalent governmental practice of management by objectives as an essential and required part of its planning effort. Beginning in the early 1970s, a number of criterion (or objectives) referenced management schemes were developed in order to help teachers manage reading skill development (see Stallard, 1977, for a listing of some 70 systems). By 1980, virtually every commercially available reading series had its own skills monitoring system. The ultimate effects of this movement may not yet be realized; nonetheless, the movement has had its most potent consequences in the proliferation of the minimal competence testing practices now mandated in several states and many large urban school districts. Whether one believes objectives referenced instruction is desirable, the success of the movement shows the extraordinary impact research and development can have.

While the empirical rational strategy may work when one introduces small changes into a large organizational unit (such as a profession), the client centered normative reeducative strategy has been shown to be effective when a change agent is attempting to introduce large scale innovation into a relatively smaller organization (such as a school or a district). A review of research in educational change, especially change requiring rather large shifts in orientation, consistently demonstrates that innovations will be accepted only if individual members of the organization are included in decision making processes as partners in a transaction. These ideas are turned into components for courses, teacher education programs, or textbooks. Similarly, open channels of communication with LEAS or the publishing industry may induce educators to make changes on their own.

It is difficult to document the separate effects of persuasive and power coercive strategies, since they are so often confounded with the other strategies. Clearly, power coercive strategies have proven effective within the past decade as different lobbying groups have persuaded state legislators or local school boards to adopt minimal competency standards for public school students and, in a few cases, undergraduates enrolled in teacher education programs. In the absence of any data supporting the efficacy of minimal competency standards, we must infer that it is the power coercive aspect of these strategies that has been effective.

The organization as the focus of change

The principal investigations in this group are the Rand Change Agent studies (Berman & McLaughlin, 1975; Emrick, 1980), the I/D/E/A studies of UCLA (Bentzen, 1974; Goodlad, 1975), the Follow Through studies (Hodges et al., 1980), the Renewal Project studies (Bassin & Gross, 1980), and the Effective School Project studies (Edmunds & Frederickson, 1979).

Gallagher, Goudvis, Pearson

The Rand study investigated the effects on schools of the adoption of four federal programs. Implementation processes, rather than student performance, served as the operational measure of program effectiveness. In summarizing the major findings, Berman and McLaughlin emphasize the importance of the local environment:

> The main factors affecting innovations were the institutional setting, particularly organizational climate and the various motivation of participants, the implementation strategy employed by local innovators to install the project treatment, and the scope of change implied by the project relative to its setting. Neither the technology nor the project resources nor the different federal management strategies influenced outcomes in major ways. Thus, project outcomes did not depend primarily on "inputs" from outside but on internal factors and local decisions. (p. 23)

The effects of other large scale programs have been investigated separately by several authors: the National Diffusion Network study (Emrick, Peterson, & Agarwala-Rogers, 1977); the Pilot-State Dissemination Project (Sieber, Louis, & Metzger, 1972); the Project Information Package program (Stearns et al., 1975, 1977). Emrick, Peterson, and Agarwala-Rogers have synthesized the major findings of all these studies:

1. Meaningful change occurs as a process, not as an event.
2. Directed personal intervention is by far the most potent technical support resource; services must be delivered to the individuals who are expected to use them.
3. The continuous personal participation of the implementing staff is needed to firmly root and sustain the utilization.
4. Administrators occupy a crucial role in supporting the utilization process.
5. Comprehensive materials resources at a "how to" level appear necessary, particularly for utilizations involving organizational or instructional change.

The UCLA I/D/E/A studies have been discussed by Bentzen (1974) and Goodlad (1975). In a five year project, an ongoing investigation of school change processes was carried out by the I/D/E/A staff in collaboration with cooperating staff members from public school systems. Beginning in 1966, a League of Cooperating Schools was formed consisting of eighteen elementary and intermediate schools spread over a nine county area in Southern California. Schools were chosen for membership in the League "so that the group would represent, as nearly as possible, a microcosm of American public schooling" (Bentzen, 1974, pp. 6-7). Gradually a process involving dialogue, decision making, action, and evaluation (DDAE) emerged as one common and helpful staff development tool. The DDAE process became the strategy for organizational change. In summarizing the I/D/E/A study findings, Lieberman (1980, p. 421) concluded:

1. The individual school is the unit of change.
2. The principal is crucially important in the change process.
3. There appears to be a process within a school staff that can be described as dialogue, decision making, and action. Schools differ markedly in the way this process is carried out.
4. The dynamics of the process appear to be a complicated set of exchanges between teachers, principals, and district personnel.
5. A supportive network of schools can create new forms for its members.

The Follow Through Planned Variation Study (see Meyer's chapter in this volume), funded by the U.S. Office of Education, has been the impetus for a significant change in elementary classrooms in a number of school districts. The Follow Through program, begun in 1967 and continuing to the present, has been a "large-scale effort to empirically test the differential effects of a range of educational models generated from the broad spectrum of educational philosophy and theory discussed in this country" (Hodges et al., 1980).

First, model sponsors developed programs representing a range of approaches to the education of young children. Sponsors were responsible for making translations of their models into practices that would work in K-3 classrooms and to install and monitor their programs in certain communities.

Hodges et al. found that the links among theory, research, and practice were most evident in the staff development and teacher training activities. They note that these efforts at on the job training are in "stark contrast to the typical preservice or inservice training of teachers in most universities, colleges, and local school systems." The procedures for training staff quickly changed from lecture type activities to active workshop training sessions, and as the years progressed, inservice training tended to become "sequential, goal directed, and continuous." They found that the training materials, the procedures for role playing in workshop settings, and the amount of direct feedback given to teachers in classroom settings were critical for successful change.

The Renewal Project studies, which began in 1969 as a cooperative effort between the New York City Board of Education and the Economic Development Council of New York City, have grown steadily to include thirty-one innercity high schools and junior highs. The primary objectives of the projects were to improve the problem solving capabilities of individual schools and to learn to make the best use possible of outside resources. Bassin and Gross (1980) suggest that the Renewal Project has succeeded in helping schools become more flexible, more receptive to innovation, and more effective in addressing their own problems.

One of the most forceful and noteworthy change efforts was undertaken by Ronald Edmonds in the late 1970s. In reviewing studies of effective schools, Edmonds and Frederickson (1979) found "unusually persuasive evidence" to confirm the thesis "that all children are eminently educable, and the behavior of the school is critical in determining the quality of that education." Edmonds and Frederickson's definition of school effectiveness is of some interest: "Our summary definition of school effectiveness required that each school eliminate the relationship between successful performance and family background." Acknowledging the popularity of the belief that the family is the principal determinant of whether a child will do well in school, Edmonds and Frederickson argue that such a belief absolves educators of their professional responsibility to be effective. They cite evidence that some schools have demonstrated that all children can be taught basic schooling skills (Brookover et al., 1978). Regardless of family background, children in the schools studied by Brookover and Lezotte achieved well beyond minimal objectives.

Edmonds and Frederickson identified five "important and indispensable" characteristics of schools in which this kind of achievement has occurred:

1. Presence of a strong leader, usually the principal, who serves as an instructional as well as an administrative leader.
2. A climate of expectation that permits no children to fall below minimum levels of achievement.
3. An atmosphere that is orderly without being oppressive, and is "generally conducive to the instructional business at hand."
4. Instructional priorities that assure that the acquisition of basic school skills takes precedence over all other school activities.
5. Standardized tests used for reporting pupil progress, for assessing what happens in classrooms, and as the basis for making changes in what is taught in the classroom.

In 1979, Edmonds was appointed by the New York City Schools to set up an Effective Schools Project. The idea of the project was to train school staffs to incorporate into their schools the five important and indispensable characteristics of schools that Edmonds and Frederickson had identified.

The project is interesting because it represents the first attempt (that we are aware of) to take the correlational findings of large scale effectiveness studies and put them into practice in an experiment involving systematic planned variations. Edmonds surveyed each school to investigate how each conformed to the profile outlined by the five important and indispensable characteristics. He and his team then set out to implement changes within the schools to help them achieve those characteristics. For example, in a school where there was no strong instructional leader, the visiting team would train the principal or some other person in that building to become a strong instructional leader. Although reports on the progress of this change effort are just becoming available, the project (which has a large amount of foundation support and the support of the New York City Chancellor's Office) is being regarded with great interest.

Summary and conclusions from organizational research. The change efforts detailed in this section lead us to conclude that schools can and do change. It is important to remind ourselves of the kind and scope of change we are considering. For the most part, these studies have been concerned with the adoption of well specified programs such as a reading curriculum in the Follow Through Studies or the Rand Studies. These programs are large, involving extensive sets of instructional procedures, prepared materials, classroom management systems, and evaluation instruments. They need to be distinguished from much smaller scale efforts that might seek to modify instructional procedures for teaching sound blending in the word identification strand of a beginning reading program.

In some of these studies, the focus has been on creating and maintaining a climate that will support a variety of specific changes while allowing appropriate modification and adaptation of prepared programs (Rand, Follow Through, UCLA I/D/E/A). In this group of studies we see the notion of mutual adaptation emerge. In others, the focus has been primarily on schools becoming generally effective rather than on adopting a specific program or prepared curriculum. What, if anything, do these various change efforts teach us about change at the organizational level?

From the studies where conducive climate was the primary objective, we learn that a normative reeducative strategy, with its emphasis on the parity of participants and interaction between concerned groups, promotes the highest degree of organizational receptivity, which in turn leads to adoption and implementation.

From the school effectiveness studies we learn that having an active and determined instructional leader is critical, as are careful monitoring of individual classrooms and informed feedback for teachers who are trying to change. These studies do not support the normative reeducative strategy as clearly as the first group. In fact, these studies support more direction from the change agent regardless of whether the agent comes from inside or outside the group. Just as the earlier group of studies triggered the term mutual adaptation to characterize successful change efforts, this group of effective school studies triggered the term directed development. This brings us to an important point: the ultimate objective of the change effort in question. If the objective is to be able to adopt a prepared program and implement it effectively, an atmosphere that promotes open discussion and cooperation appears to be essential. On the other hand, if the objective is to alter the expectations and attendant behaviors of a school staff in a fundamental way, strong, directive leadership is essential.

In the long run, we may find that mutual adaptation and directed development can be used in different phases of the same project. For example, a principal who has achieved a satisfactory level of overall effectiveness may begin to yield some authority to the teachers. In this way, the relative dominance of centralized leadership and authority (directed development) may give way to the more democratic, cooperative effort that is characteristic of the first set of findings (mutual adaptation).

From many studies we have learned that change efforts are best centered in individual buildings, in which faculty members feel they can improve their capabilities as problem solvers and planners. When outside programs are adopted, the most important determinant of implementation success is the level of receptivity within the school. In terms of strategies, these data tend to support a normative reeducative strategy with its emphasis on parity of participants and transaction among forces for change; however, some elements of the power coercive and persuasive strategies emerge from the directed development efforts.

Teaching as the focus of change

While large scale change efforts focus on an entire school or even a school district, professional development programs designate the teacher as the focus of change efforts. When the focus of change is on the individual classroom or the teacher, rather than the entire organization, we can draw on the professional development literature and on experimental studies that seek to promote specific changes in teacher behavior. Professional development (also commonly referred to as staff development or inservice) has change as its most general goal, but often the kind of change in question is very specific and restricted in generality (e.g., improved techniques for teaching story writing or alternatives for math facts drill). Here we are no longer concerned exclusively with studying how change occurs but also with attempts to bring about specific changes.

When teaching is the focus of change, there are two key issues to be considered. One is the voice individual teachers have in determining the course of their own professional development. The other concerns anticipated outcomes of professional development activities. What are they supposed to accomplish?

When people write critically about professional development, they often begin with the observation that professional development is determined centrally, with little or no input from teachers. Though this is a common perception, there is little evidence that it is true.

The second consideration forces us to question the goals of many professional development efforts. As a hypothetical case in point, we can think of a school district that has decided its math program needs some shoring up. A common practice would be for the curriculum coordinator (or assistant superintendent) to schedule throughout the year five workshops on math instruction. However, the curriculum coordinator, with or without the input of the teachers, may fail to develop any expectations about the specific direction of changes in instruction that teachers should make. Further, there is likely to be no provision for thorough follow up or support for teachers attempting to try these changes. Few class visits will be made; little or no feedback will be offered. Rarely will teachers see an actual demonstration of the kind of instruction promoted in the inservice sessions.

We are referring here to the vagueness that permeates most discussion of professional development programs. The problem with vagueness is evident in many states and schools. For example, most states mandate a predetermined number of days in each school year to be devoted to teachers' professional development. A familiar pattern for these institute days is a smorgasbord of interesting but unrelated (either to each other or to any documented curricular needs) sessions. It is not surprising, then, that many people view such efforts as having little impact on the quality of classroom instruction.

Teacher centered professional development. In response to the conventional perception that most professional development efforts have been imposed upon teachers without their input, much of the recent work in professional development has focused on making teachers active participants in determining their own professional development (see Rubin, 1978).

There is evidence to support involving teachers in determining the course of their own professional development. Lawrence (in Rubin, 1978) examined 97 studies of continuing teacher education programs and drew several conclusions about successful inservice programs. Success was more likely when teachers planned and worked together to implement the activities than when programs were conducted by people outside the school system without the involvement of local personnel. Success also depended on designing programs that responded to teachers' perceived needs and individual interests rather than the interests of a large, diverse group. Finally, success was more likely if the inservice program went beyond the typical one shot presentation of ideas and techniques to include opportunities for teachers to try out new ideas and obtain feedback about how well they were implementing new techniques.

Since the early 1970s there have been a number of attempts to address the question of how to help teachers become more involved in setting the agenda for their own professional development. Some of the most visible attempts to inspire educators to examine, and perhaps change, their teaching came from the teacher center "movement" of the late 1960s and 1970s. Devaney (1977) distinguishes several differences between traditional inservice/staff development programs and teacher centers. First, teacher centers are voluntary organizations rather than required programs. Second, teacher centers try to *respond to* rather than *direct* teachers' expressed needs and interests. There is no single curriculum being promoted or technique being offered. Traditional inservice programs presented to teachers, rather than organized by teachers, seldom focus on the in-

Gallagher, Goudvis, Pearson

dividual teacher's classroom concerns. On the other hand, these concerns are the primary focus of teacher center work, with instructional materials and classroom procedures assuming paramount importance. This emphasis on the individual teacher's selection and construction of materials encourages teachers to assume greater responsibility and control of the classroom curriculum.

A similar effort has been undertaken by the Workshop Center for Open Education associated with the School of Education at City College in New York. Through its affiliation with the School of Education, the Workshop Center plays a part in preservice as well as inservice teacher education. Again, the emphasis is on providing opportunities for teachers and others involved in the educational enterprise to learn from one another; to improve and refine classroom curricula; and to broaden professional horizons in a well staffed, well equipped environment. (See Alberty, Webber, & Neujahr, 1983, for a description of Workshop Center activities in the past decade.)

Another less well documented effort in this vein is represented by the advisory model of professional development. In the advisory model, teachers work individually with an advisor (usually another teacher) to clarify purposes, refine teaching practices, and evaluate effectiveness. One of the distinctive features of the advisory model is the attention to individual teachers and their own classrooms, sustained over a long period of time. (See Katz, 1979, and Thomas, 1980, for a more detailed description.)

A second approach for involving teachers in their own professional development is the collaborative research movement. The rationale underlying this approach is straightforward. In classroom level action research projects, problem solving orientation is the most critical characteristic of a teacher who can respond to the continually shifting constraints operating in the classroom environment.

Teachers are confronted with continually changing factors in the classroom. To be effective, teachers must develop skills that allow them to respond flexibly to always changing conditions. They do not need a new prepackaged curriculum; they need general problem solving orientation to direct their decision making. Those who advocate the collaborative research paradigm believe the best way to help teachers develop and refine problem solving orientation is by teaching them to conduct research studies in their own classrooms.

This approach assumes that the data available to teachers on a daily basis are just as informative for making real decisions about teaching and learning as are published curriculum guides, expert advice, teacher's manuals, or an administrative mandate. The spirit of this approach is captured by the phrase, "Teaching as a continuing experiment."

The earliest reference we could find promoting this approach is the work of Barnes in the 1950s (Barnes, 1964), although it is certainly consistent with the philosophical views of Dewey and Lewin. There have been several efforts fostering collaborative research. The most ambitious effort took place at Michigan State University's Institute for Research on Teaching (IRT).

At the IRT, local educators can and do become teacher collaborators who participate in a wide range of school based research projects. Writing about this sort of collaboration, Shallaway and Lanier (1978) point out that parity between IRT researchers and teachers is important; consequently, responsibilities for the projects are shared. At the same time, there is a conviction that both researchers and teachers have different vantage points and should work to maintain distinct perspectives.

On a smaller scale, the work of Carol Santa in the Kalispell, Montana, Public Schools (see Chapter 9, this volume) and the Metcalf Project (see Chapter 10, this volume) are examples of recent collaborative research projects.

Curriculum centered professional development. While much recent energy has gone into the teacher centered approaches to professional development, there is an accumulating body of research that is not specifically designed to describe *how* to help teachers change, but does permit us to draw some conclusions about strategies that are successful when the focus of the change is centered on the curriculum rather than the individual teacher.

We were able to locate five studies growing out of the effective teaching tradition (Brophy, 1982). In most of the studies, by reviewing teacher effectiveness research, the researcher identified

Gallagher, Goudvis, Pearson

specific behaviors used by effective teachers but not by their less effective peers (where effectiveness is determined by scores on standardized tests). Through what resembled conventional inservice techniques, the researchers tried to help teachers adopt the strategies used by effective teachers.

These successful small scale programs include improving mathematics instruction (Good & Grouws, 1979a, 1979b), problem solving skills (Grouws & Thomas, 1981), reading instruction and classroom management (Anderson, Evertson, & Brophy, 1979), and specific reading skills (Stallings, 1978). In each case, the investigators were successful in modifying teacher behavior, as measured by direct observation. In the four studies where student achievement was the goal, the experimental groups were superior to control groups of students; where student engagement was the goal, experimental teachers were superior to control teachers.

In four of the studies, teacher training was minimal. Training was guided by brief presentations of basic instructional principles to be used and booklets that outlined the specific teaching procedures. Direct observation provided evidence that the teachers did change their behavior in the suggested manner, even though they were not exposed to intensive training.

The evidence provided by the curriculum centered studies suggests that a rational empirical strategy is effective when applied to certain individual oriented models of change for small scale programs. Teachers in these studies did assimilate and apply ideas stemming directly from research efforts, and they did so with inservice that amounted to little more than providing information that teachers could gain from a journal article.

There also have been some large scale curriculum centered change efforts. In a summary paper of five large scale studies of educational change and dissemination, Emrick (1980) posits some implications for professional development programs. He concludes that schools and practitioners may be much more amenable to change than has been assumed in the past, provided the context of a given situation and the practitioner as an individual are considered important factors in the change process. While administrators and exemplary staff members play important roles in whatever changes occur in schools, Emrick concludes that practitioners themselves should participate in decision making activities in the schools, carrying out problem solving, staff development, and program improvement activities.

According to McLaughlin (1977), any approach to professional development is based on underlying assumptions about teacher training and development. The Rand study indicates that one view of teacher development is a deficit model, in which teachers are viewed as needing improved techniques and methods. McLaughlin suggests that the development model, which tries to give teachers the skills to identify and solve problems themselves, is clearly the more successful approach to staff development.

During the course of the Rand study, McLaughlin and her coinvestigators were concerned about how their conclusions might transfer to existing staff development programs. This led to a followup study of five districts and some conclusions about characteristics which lead to effective staff development programs. Among these were the importance of the district's attitude toward teachers as responsible professionals capable of and interested in helping to plan and implement inservice and staff development programs. Another conclusion was that districts with programs based on the inadequacies of both teachers and the instructional program also had little staff input into professional development activities, with a resulting program in which there was a noticeable lack of interest and involvement. McLaughlin cites the presence of six practices in districts where professional development was determined to be effective:

1. There was an attitude within the district that viewed teachers as capable of directing their own professional development.
2. Teacher centers had been organized as informal places for staff to work on curricular materials and share ideas.
3. There was no districtwide inservice/staff development program in operation.
4. Local resource people (rather than outside experts) guided innovative efforts.
5. There was joint governing by administrators and teachers on staff development issues.

Gallagher, Goudvis, Pearson

6. Released time was acknowledged as an important part of the staff development program.

While these few examples illustrate what researchers studying professional development programs believe should exist (rather than what does exist), there are indications that professional development programs are moving in the direction of providing practitioners with greater responsibility for their own professional development.

Summary and conclusions: Focus on teaching. What have we learned from our discussion of teaching as the focus of change? Our review suggests there is widespread consensus on two points. First, most professional development programs available to teachers are too vague with respect to goals and procedures. Second, individual teachers' interests and needs must be taken into account during the planning of professional development programs.

While there is little research documenting the effectiveness (as measured by either teacher satisfaction or student achievement) of teacher centered professional development, the recent flurry of activities in this vein attests to both its appeal and its potential. Ironically, the only well documented efforts (the curriculum centered studies) have demonstrated little concern for individual teacher interests or needs.

We do not know what made change possible – what produced the climate for allowing this type of change to occur. One distinction we should make is the difference between general receptivity and the willingness and ability to adopt specific procedures that may displace other equally specific procedures. It is worth noting here that many instructional intervention studies yield positive results at this same level of specificity (Pearson & Gallagher, 1983).

Coda

So far we have introduced four generic change strategies (rational empirical, normative reeducative, power coercive, and persuasive), discussed a body of research focusing on organizations that yielded two postures toward change (mutual adaptation and directed development), and considered literature concerning teaching as the focus of change that yielded a distinction about the target of change efforts (the teacher or the curriculum). The question is, how does this array of concepts fit together to help us understand issues in educational change and draw conclusions about what each of us might try in our own particular circumstances? To this end, we have tried to derive some conclusions about the phenomenon of change and some advice to those about to embark on change efforts.

First, the conclusions:

1. All the distinctions we have made among postures, foci, and different strategies tend to cluster into patterns of relationship (covariation) as depicted in the Figure. On average, a directed development posture tends to be associated with a curriculum focus, while a mutual adaptation posture tends to be associated with a teacher focus. The primary change strategies within directed development tend to be either power coercive or persuasive; in other words, the impetus for and direction of change tends to be mandated from the top down. By contrast, the normative reeducative strategy is the primary strategy within mutual adaptation; the first task is to help teachers determine how and why they might want to change.

Patterns of covariation among postures, foci, and strategies in intentional efforts for change

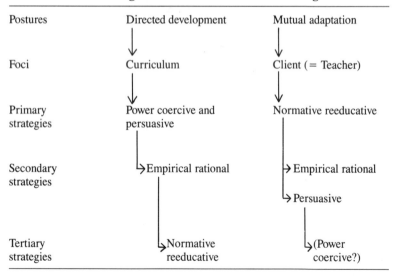

Postures	Directed development	Mutual adaptation
Foci	Curriculum	Client (= Teacher)
Primary strategies	Power coercive and persuasive	Normative reeducative
Secondary strategies	→ Empirical rational	→ Empirical rational
		→ Persuasive
Tertiary strategies	→ Normative reeducative	→ (Power coercive?)

Gallagher, Goudvis, Pearson

Within both postures, the empirical rational strategy emerges as a secondary change strategy, usually realized as dissemination activity in the form of workshops or readings; additionally, persuasive strategies arise within the mutual adaption posture in this second tier of strategies. As a tertiary strategy, the normative reeducative strategy plays a role in directed development postures, as change agents try to instill project ownership within the clients. We doubt that power coercive strategies ever can be a part of mutual adaption (hence the parentheses and ? in the Figure), because authoritarian activities are inherently inconsistent with the notion of parity among participants so characteristic of the mutual adaption posture. Finally, a basic distinction can be made between these two postures: Directed development tends to work in a top down (from authority to teacher) fashion; mutual adaptation, in a bottom up (from the teacher upward) fashion.

2. There is merit in the age old empirical rational tradition. If you have the patience of Job and are willing to wait a decade or a quarter century, then you can achieve change simply through straightforward dissemination activities. The change will be diffuse and the implementation will vary dramatically from one context to another, but it can be achieved.

3. If you want people to make only minor shifts in orientation or behavior, again you can accomplish your aims through relatively simple straightforward professional development devices like workshops or manuals. The consumers need only to see the usefulness of the change in order to embrace it.

4. If you want the people in an organization, like a school, to change dramatically—to make major shifts in orientation or behavior—you have to adopt a problem solving, transactive, client centered approach. In other words, you have to move into the normative reeducative tradition. The consumers need to recognize the need for change and be heavily involved in planning and implementing it. The change effort will not succeed without strong leadership within the organization. Teachers (the consumers) have to be assured that the changes are desirable within the school system's incentive structure, and all parties must feel ownership of the effort. And the change agents must work with the clients (i.e., teachers) who are

most directly involved in implementing the actual changes (see Meyer, Chapter 3, this volume for a convincing argument).

Now the advice to those charged with implementing change:

1. Read the rest of this volume, especially the case studies of change efforts in Part 2, for the specific and contextually rooted advice of those who have done it will be more useful to those charged with implementing change than will our broad generalizations.

2. Successful change can result from either directed development or mutual adaptation, as long as you make sure the two key elements are present — ownership and knowledge. In the final analysis, you cannot force anyone to change. Ultimately, teachers have enough autonomy to circumvent or undermine virtually any mandate you might impose. Ownership must be established in order for any change to survive. Equally important is the quality of the knowledge that is the basis for change. At times, bad or misguided knowledge seems to have too much currency in our schools; ultimately, however, knowledge supported by logic and evidence and blessed by the practical wisdom of teaching (it works in real classrooms!) will rise to the top. Also, teachers will recognize bogus information and find ways to ignore it.

3. Establish a climate where the expectation for change is the norm rather than the exception. The real goal can never be to implement a particular change, one that will become as entrenched as the conventional wisdom it was designed to replace. Instead, the real goal must be to establish a mechanism for continual renewal. As you read the chapters in Part 2, you will discover that most of our successful case studies in change focus more on the *process* of change than they do on the *product* of change. There always will be better ideas and better knowledge. But unless you have established a process to allow those ideas to ease into your curricular program, they may never have an impact on your teachers and students.

We close with both a word of caution and a glimmer of hope. The caution is this: If we are not able to work together using the friendly principles of change inherent in empirical rational and normative reeducative strategies for change, we will become the victims of forces within and outside the educational community that favor less friendly power coercive strategies to force us to change in

Gallagher, Goudvis, Pearson

ways we know are either wrong or misguided. The recent flurry of national reports on the ills of education and the accompanying push for new standards of excellence (which the proponents typically want to put into law) bear testimony to the real likelihood of forced change.

The glimmer of hope is embodied in the remainder of this volume. We believe that our colleagues have provided you with sensible, practical, and professionally nurturing examples of how educators can work together to bring about change that is more helpful and more durable than any that could ever be brought into existence by the hostile forces of coercion.

References

Alberty, B., Webber, L., and Neujahr, J. *Taking root: The workshop center at city college.* New York: School of Education, City College of CUNY, 1982.

Anderson, L.M., Evertson, C.M., and Brophy, J.E. An experimental study of effective teaching in first grade reading groups. *Elementary School Journal, 1979, 79.*

Barnes, Fred P. *Research for the practitioner in education.* Washington, DC: Department of Elementary School Principals, 1964.

Bassin, M., and Gross, T. Turning on big city schools: Pragmatic participatory problem solving. In M.M. Milstein (Ed.), *Schools, conflict, and change.* New York: Columbia University, Teachers College Press, 1980.

Bennis, W.G., Benne, K.D., and Chin, R. (Eds.). *The planning of change,* second edition. New York: Holt, Rinehart & Winston, 1969.

Bentzen, M. *Changing schools: The magic feather principle.* New York: McGraw-Hill, 1974.

Berman, P., and McLaughlin, M.W. *Federal programs supporting educational change,* volume 4: *The findings in review.* Santa Monica, CA: Rand, 1975.

Bloom, B.S. *Learning for mastery.* Los Angeles: University of California, Center for the Study of Evaluation of Instructional Programs, 1968.

Bond, G.L., and Dykstra, R. The cooperative research program in first grade reading instruction. *Reading Research Quarterly, 1967, 2, 4.*

Bradford, L.P., Benne, K.D., and Gibb, J.R. *T-group theory and laboratory method.* New York: Wiley, 1964.

Brookover, W.B., Schweitzer, J.H., Schneider, J., Beady, C.H., Flood, P.K., and Wisenbaker, J.M. Elementary school social climate and school achievement. *American Educational Research Journal, 1978, 15,* 301-318.

Brophy, J.E. Successful teaching strategies for the innercity child. *Phi Delta Kappan, 1982, 63.*

Chall, J. *Learning to read: The great debate.* New York: McGraw-Hill, 1967.

Chin, R., and Benne, K.D. General strategies for effecting changes in human systems. In W.G. Bennis, K.D. Benne, and R. Chin (Eds.), *The planning of change,* second edition. New York: Holt, Rinehart & Winston, 1969.

Clifford, G.J. Words for schools: The applications in education of the vocabulary researches of Edward L. Thorndike. In I.P. Suppes (Ed.), *Impact of research on education: Some case studies.* Washington, DC: National Academy of Education, 1978.

Devaney, K. *Essays on teachers' centers.* San Francisco: Far West Laboratory for Educational Research and Development, 1977.

Dewey, J. *Philosophy, psychology, and social practice.* New York: Capricorn Books, 1967.

Edmonds, R., and Frederickson, J.R. *Search for effective schools: The identification and analysis of city schools that are instructionally effective for poor children.* New York: Board of Education, 1979.

Emrick, J.A. Some implications of recent research on educational dissemination and change for teacher education (inservice) programs. In G.E. Hall, S.M. Hord, and G. Brown (Eds.), *Exploring issues in teacher education: Questions for future research.* Austin, TX: University of Texas, Research and Development Center for Teacher Education, 1980.

Emrick, J.A., Peterson, S.M., and Agarwala-Rogers, R. *Evaluation of the national diffusion network.* Menlo Park, CA: Stanford Research Institute, 1977.

Freud, S. *An outline of psychoanalysis,* revised edition. New York: Norton, 1972 (originally published, 1949).

Gagne, R.M. *The conditions of learning,* second edition. New York: Holt, Rinehart & Winston, 1970.

Gagne, R.M. (Ed.). *Learning and individual differences.* Columbus, OH: Merrill, 1967.

Glaser, R. Instructional technology and the measure of learning outcomes. In D.A. Payne and R.F. McMorris (Eds.), *Educational and psychological measurement.* Waltham, MA: Blaisdell, 1967.

Good, J.L., and Grouws, D.A. The Missouri mathematics effectiveness project: An experimental study in fourth grade classrooms. *Journal of Educational Psychology,* 1979, *71,* 355-362.

Good, J.L., and Grouws, D.A. *Experimental study of mathematics instruction in elementary schools.* Columbia, MO: University of Missouri, College of Education, 1979.

Goodlad, J.I. *The dynamics of educational change: Toward responsive schools.* New York: McGraw-Hill, 1975.

Grouws, D., and Thomas, W.E. Problem solving: A panoramic approach. *School Science and Mathematics,* 1981, *81,* 307-314.

Havelock, R.G., and Benne, K.D. An exploratory study of knowledge utilization. In W.G. Bennis, K.D. Benne, and R. Chin (Eds.), *The planning of change,* second edition. New York: Holt, Rinehart & Winston, 1969.

Havelock, R.G., and Havelock, M.C. *Training for change agents.* Ann Arbor, MI: University of Michigan Institute for Social Research, 1973.

Hodges, W., Branden, A., Feldman, R., Follins, J., Love, J., Sheehan, R., Lumbley, J., Osborn, J., Renfrow, R.K., Houston, J., and Lee, C. *Forces for change in the primary schools.* Ypsilanti, MI: High/Scope Press, 1980.

Katz, L. *Helping others learn to teach: Some principles and techniques for inservice educators.* Urbana, IL: ERIC Clearinghouse on Early Childhood Education, 1979.

Lewin, K. *Field theory in social science.* New York: Harper & Row, 1951.

Lieberman, A. Describers and improvers: People, processes, and problems. In G.E. Hall, S.M. Hord, and G. Brown (Eds.), *Exploring issues in teacher education: Questions for future research.* Austin, TX: University of Texas Research and Development Center for Teacher Education, 1980.

Lippitt, R. The process of utilization of social research to improve social practice. In W.G. Bennis, K.D. Benne, and R. Chin (Eds.), *The planning of change,* second edition. New York: Holt, Rinehart & Winston.

Mager, R.F. *Preparing instructional objectives.* San Francisco, CA: Fearon, 1962.

McLaughlin, M.W. Pygmalion in the school district: Issues for staff development programs. In K. Devaney (Ed.), *Essays on teachers' centers.* San Francisco, CA: Far West Laboratory for Educational Research and Development, 1977.

Morrish, I. *Aspects of educational change.* New York: Wiley, 1976.

Pearson, P.D., and Gallagher, M.C. *The instruction of reading comprehension.* Technical Report No. 297. Urbana, IL: University of Illinois, Center for the Study of Reading, 1983.

Popham, W.J., Eisner, E.W., Sullivan, H.J., and Tyler, L.L. Instructional objectives. *AERA monograph series on curriculum evaluation,* No. 3. Chicago: Rand McNally, 1969.

Rubin, L. *Inservice education of teachers: Trends, processes, and prescriptions.* Boston: Allyn & Bacon, 1978.

Shallaway, L., and Lanier, J. *Teachers attaining new roles in research: A challenge to the educational community.* East Lansing, MI: Michigan State University, Institute for Research on Teaching, 1978.

Sieber, S.D., Louis, R.S., and Metzger, L. *The use of educational knowledge: Evaluation of the pilot state dissemination program.* New York: Columbia University, Bureau of Applied Social Research, 1972. (ED 065 740)

Stallard, C. Comparing objective based reading programs. *Journal of Reading,* 1977, *21.*

Stallings, J.A. *Teaching basic reading skills in secondary schools.* Menlo Park, CA: SRI International, 1978.

Stearns, M.S. et al. *Evaluation of the field test of Project Information Packs.* Menlo Park, CA: Stanford Research Institute and RMC Research, 1975, 1977.

Thomas, G. Advisor: Long-term supporter of teachers. *Thrust for Educational Leadership,* 1980, *9,* 21-24.

Zaltman, G., and Duncan, R. *Strategies for planned change.* New York: Wiley, 1977.

Zaltman, G., Florio, D., and Sikorski, L.A. *Dynamic educational change.* New York: Free Press, 1977.

Prelude

B *efore coming to the Center for the Study of Reading at the University of Illinois, Linda Meyer spent several years working as a consultant and researcher on the Follow Through Studies. She continues to study the processes by which teachers and change agents adapt to innovation. In this chapter, she challenges some of the holy grails of research on change; she suggests there are alternative interpretations to the conclusions drawn by Berman and McLaughlin in their influential Rand Report on institutional change. She argues strongly for what has come to be known as the directed development model of change (one in which the change agents maintain substantial control) as superior to the mutual adaptation model.*

3

Research on implementation:
What seems to work

An urban school district superintendent wants to increase the percentage of students reading at or above grade level. She assumes she will have to make changes in instructional programs. What should she do? Should she mandate new teaching schedules? Should she assess needs to determine what others feel are priorities? Should she rely exclusively on personnel already in her district, or should she bring in experts to help make decisions?

All of these questions face school administrators and supervisors who want to change something in their schools. At one extreme, administrators can mandate change, while at the other extreme they can allow teachers to choose what to do and how to do it. A more moderate position is mutual adaptation, a process whereby teachers and others plan together to develop strategies for change. How effective is mutual adaptation? Is there one strategy for producing change that has the best chance to succeed? And, what does *success* mean?

Questions about what strategy to use are hard to answer. Although a lot has been written about models, or theories, of change, few persons have studied change strategies carefully enough to make general conclusions about the superiority of one method over any other. Despite this, mutual adaptation is often suggested as the best way for administrators to bring about changes in their schools.

What we know on a pragmatic level about successful change strategies comes primarily from projects funded by the federal government to help poor, minority students. Most of these studies began during the 1960s as part of the War on Poverty. This chapter presents the theoretical definition of mutual adaptation and then applies the definition to several large scale change efforts to see if change agents and their clients practiced mutual adaptation as they implemented their programs.

The basis for mutual adaptation

With the beginning of the War on Poverty, projects such as Head Start, Follow Through, and Experience Based Career Education emerged as major educational experiments for disadvantaged youth from preschool age through high school. These efforts provided opportunities to study how institutions implementing these programs changed and how the individuals involved perceived the changes. Numerous papers document each program's success or failure (see Rivlin & Timpane, 1976, and Weikart & Banet, 1975, for articles on Follow Through), while others (Zimiles, Mayer, & Wickens, 1980; Zoref, 1981) describe the processes the schools or school districts went through to implement change.

The most widely cited document of this era is the Rand Report (Berman & McLaughlin, 1975), a report that describes the change process in four large, federally supported programs. One of the Report's major conclusions is that "An implementation strategy that promotes mutual adaptation is critical" (p. x).

The impact of this report has been substantial. Researchers and administrators have accepted mutual adaptation as the best way to achieve educational change. But results from attempts to use this strategy cast doubts on the validity and success of the mutual adaptation process and its outcomes. Why? To answer this question, we must look at the program reports Berman and McLaughlin studied to see if their conclusions seem warranted. We also must look at later attempts to use mutual adaptation to see if that strategy worked.

Mutual adaptation: Is there such a thing?

One large program that used mutual adaptation was Experience Based Career Education (EBCE). EBCE was intended "to make education more relevant by getting students out of school and into the world of 'real experience' " (Farrar, DeSanctis, & Cohen, 1980a). EBCE was sponsored by four laboratories, each of which developed EBCE models during the mid 1970s. The laboratories then implemented their effective models, so that by 1978 EBCE was disseminated to almost every state.

The Farrar, DeSanctis, and Cohen report on the overall implementation of EBCE describes the mutual adaptation process as "marked by controversy, negotiation, revision, and adaptation" (p. 85). They further explained that in some schools or districts, entire components of models were not implemented and that adaptation was seldom mutual. Sponsors usually compromised their models to meet schools' requests.

Farrar, DeSanctis, and Cohen also report views of EBCE from staff, nonstaff, administrators, school board members, and principals in their studies of the implementation efforts. These views are summarized as follows.

EBCE staff. Staff views varied widely. Some viewed EBCE as an opportunity to work with smaller groups of students on social skills or individual basic skills, while others used the opportunity to do more counseling or tutoring. Many administrators and teachers simply ignored career guidance—the mission of the project. Some teachers were resistant, others enjoyed newfound freedom. In short, there was great variety in what teachers did and how they felt about Experience Based Career Education.

Non EBCE staff. There was general resentment toward the program by non EBCE staff, although some teachers recognized the need for such a program. Some teachers and administrators liked to be able to "dump" their lowest performing students into EBCE.

Administrators and school board members. The general motives of administrators and school board members who became involved in EBCE ranged from financial incentives to concerns about the image of their school districts. Still others were concerned about recruiting students to integrate a school. In many ways, administrators' and school board members' views were similar to teachers' views—there was wide variation from one person to another.

School principals. EBCE principals also held a wide range of views about the project. Some supported it and wanted all of their students in the program. Some described it as a headache or nuisance. Farrar, DeSanctis, and Cohen (1980a, p. 93) concluded, "Like others directly concerned with implementation, principals bring their personal and professional agendas to the innovation, seek out the features most salient to them, improvise accordingly, and so contribute to the local variation that evolves."

Thus, EBCE staff, administrators, school board members, principals, and non EBCE staff had very different views of the program. Their views ranged from positive attitudes toward the opportunity to work more closely with individual students or better meet the needs of "difficult" students to negative attitudes about something new and different.

After Farrar, DeSanctis, and Cohen reported these various positions, they speculated that these diverse views may have existed because the strength of local conditions overpowered the weaker federal influence. Another explanation offered was that participation in the program was voluntary. Farrar and her colleagues also pointed out that for many federal programs "while there is some monitoring, it is often sporadic and little more than ritual" (p. 94); the local education agencies are basically independent and are incapable of directing change from the top down; the sponsor groups, not the school personnel, did the adapting. Therefore, there was little or no mutual adaptation. After reading the report of Farrar and her colleagues, one is left with the impression that the EBCE program implementations were quite variable and that attempts at mutual adaptation frequently resulted in divergent programs that lacked common purposes and commitments.

Mutual adaptation revisited

In a similar study, Kennedy (1978) reanalyzed the Follow Through data in order to study variation in site performance. (Follow Through was a federally funded K-3 project with planned variation in about 150 communities in the United States.) Kennedy determined that one critical difference between successful and unsuccessful sponsors was the amount of technical assistance experts gave directly to the classroom teachers in their projects.

Meanwhile, Datta (1980, 1981) reanalyzed the data and conclusions in the Rand Report (Berman & McLaughlin, 1975). In her 1980 work, Datta traced three beliefs about change that had emerged since the mid 1960s: (1) There should be a systematic, long term change process (Weikart & Banet, 1975); (2) schools should manage themselves by first anaylzing their needs and then monitoring their changes (Goodlad, 1975; Havelock, 1973; Schmuck et al., 1977); and (3) schools are so loosely coupled that change at one level will not necessarily filter to another level.

A year later, Datta suggested that "the programs studied [for the Rand Report] were not examples of massive funds for innovation...nor of implementing innovations of proven effectiveness, nor of enormous infusions of technical expertise" (Datta, 1981, p. 28). When Datta reviewed the regulations for programs studied by Berman and McLaughlin, she found that the guidelines required the 293 projects to encourage development of model school programs (ESEA Title III), develop diagnostic/prescriptive reading (Right to Read), produce demonstration grants (Vocational Education Act, 1963), or develop exemplary bilingual programs (ESEA Title VII). The key words in all of these regulations were *develop, produce,* or synonyms requiring participants to come up with unique programs. The point is that mutual adaptation seems to have grown from work not even designed to be innovative.

In light of these reanalyses, Datta suggested that so little is actually known about implementation that much of the current literature can best be described as "fantasizing about how change occurs" (Datta, 1980, p. 102). In addition, Datta questioned the factor analytic methods Berman and McLaughlin used to reduce twenty-eight methods to five program scores. Furthermore, she concluded that the eight volume Rand Report rejected the help of "experts" without either defining or describing technical assistance. A startling finding reported by teachers in the projects was that almost one third (29 percent) seldom received help during the first year of the program. In fact, only slightly more than half (58 percent) of the teachers reported attending "some" meetings on their project. Did the other 13 percent even know they were supposed to be doing anything different? In short, most of these teachers received little if any help. Datta further states that even under these less than ideal conditions, the difference in perceived usefulness just slightly favors local assistance over expert assistance.

The Rand Report also found that teachers' willingness to accept change was influenced by the usefulness of the help they received and by the relationship between consultant help and total student improvement. In other words, changes in the teachers' own behavior that resulted in improved student performance seemed to matter most. Datta found that number of years as a teacher, teacher effectiveness, and support for training did not account for differences among schools. In addition, the extra money provided by the programs was apparently unimportant in their implementation or effectiveness. If anything, these reanalyses support the need for use of outside experts and directed development instead of supporting local decision making and implementation strategies.

What might this mean to school personnel? It is interesting and encouraging that the reanalyses of Follow Through by Kennedy (1978) and of the Rand Report by Datta (1980, 1981) support the need for some kind of directed development and pragmatic help from experts in school districts with large numbers of disadvantaged students. These findings are also supported by empirical research in math (Good & Grouws, 1979), remedial reading (Stallings, 1980), and classroom management (Anderson, Evertson, & Brophy, 1979).

Further support for a directed development strategy emerged from two additional projects. The next part of this chapter will focus on the School Improvement Project (SIP) in New York City and on the second year of an implementation study of a Direct Instruction Follow Through site. These descriptions are elaborate because both studies involve a number of questions about change. The detail is presented to illustrate the complexity of the issues involved in changing behavior in the field of education. The detail also illustrates that it is possible to quantify at least some aspects of the change process. (An even more detailed description of what went on in these settings appears in Meyer, 1983.)

Recent large scale change efforts

New York City: School Improvement Project

In 1979 the New York City Public Schools received funding from the Carnegie Corporation and the Ford Foundation for technical assistance to implement findings from the research on effective schools (Edmonds, 1979). The SIP focused on administrative leadership, instruction in basic skills, school climate, ongoing assessment of pupil progress, and teacher expectations. The primary goal was to work with schools in New York City, first assessing a school's needs in each of the areas mentioned and then working to improve the school in the areas identified in the needs assessment. The following data summary is based on the Third Annual Process Evaluation (McCarthy et al., 1982).

The schools. Nineteen public and five private elementary schools in New York City participated. Seven of the public schools were in SIP for their third year (Cohort 1), eight for their second year (Cohort 2), and four were new to SIP (Cohort 3). Each of the schools met three criteria for inclusion in the project: the principals volunteered, school needs and the goals of the project meshed, and there were no other ongoing school development projects in the schools.

The liaisons. Each school had a liaison assigned from the Central Board of Education to assist in the needs assessment for the school and to support other phases of the project. The data for this report were gathered from principals, assistant principals, teachers, paraprofessionals, auxiliary staff, and parents. Data were collected from interviews or questionnaires. Student achievement data for the five school years prior to this intervention as well as student achievement data for the years of the school's participation in SIP were collected from each school to serve as measures of the effectiveness of change.

Documentation unit. The documentation unit from the Central Board of Education kept ongoing records of the interviews from the liaisons' logs and other minutes, notes, statistical student data, and project documents. This unit developed reports at the end of each of the three years of SIP.

Interviews and questionnaires. The staff from the documentation unit conducted three structured interviews with administrators, liaisons, and principals. Two forced choice (yes or no) questionnaires were administered. The first questionnaire dealt with twenty-three questions pertaining to the committee to plan the school improvement tasks. The second questionnaire went schoolwide to everyone. The rate of return for this questionnaire was 84 percent for Cohort 1, 84 percent for Cohort 2, and 75 percent for Cohort 3.

Findings from the School Improvement Project

The Table shows the strategies Cohort 1 and Cohort 2 schools implemented to improve the five variables studied: administrative leadership, improving basic skills, improving school climate, improving ongoing assessment, and teacher expectations. (Cohort 3 implementation data are not available.)

There are several interesting patterns in the strategies used to improve the SIP schools. For each cohort, a strategy was judged successful if it was implemented, regardless of its effect on student achievement. Strategies to improve administrative leadership were judged about equally successful for Cohort 1 and Cohort 2, although only Cohort 2 schools tried instructional materials management. Instructional materials management and materials changes together show an increase in management and control from the first to the second cohort.

Similar patterns are present in improving basic skills. The most successfully implemented strategies are the ones that directly affect students—parent tutors and allocated time increases.

Of the seven types of strategies attempted in improving school climate, five tried by Cohort 2 were implemented more successfully than those attempted by Cohort 1. All of these strategies involved things other than changes to the physical plant.

The final two areas, improving ongoing assessment and teacher expectations, also show rather clear patterns for strategies involving order and direction.

SIP ratings of the success of school change strategies in nineteen schools

Change variable	Cohort 1	Cohort 2
Administrative leadership		
Materials changes	3.00	3.00
Communication	3.00	2.50
Organizational changes	3.00	2.30
Physical plant changes	3.00	3.00
Instructional materials management	–	2.28
Improving basic skills		
Materials changes	3.00	2.50
Workshops with experts	2.80	2.25
Parent tutors	–	3.33
Allocated time increases	3.00	3.33
Space allocation changes	2.00	–
Improving school climate		
Changes to the physical plant	4.00	2.30
Assemblies and get togethers	2.75	3.50
Parent/school involvement	2.00	2.80
Schedule changes	2.00	3.00
Behavior programs	–	2.60
Relaxation program	3.00	–
Communication program	–	3.00
Improving ongoing assessment		
Workshops	2.67	2.33
Coverage tracking	3.00	3.00
Criterion referenced assessment	–	3.00
Studying test scores	–	3.00
Teachers' access to test scores	–	3.00
Teacher expectations		
Student recognition programs	–	3.00
Goal setting	–	2.00
Workshops	–	3.00
Positive feedback	–	2.00

4 = Very successful
3 = Successful
2 = Somewhat successful
1 = Slightly successful
0 = Not at all successful

Overall, direction from experts increased over the years of SIP implementation, as evidenced in the move to specify the instructional materials after the first year. Furthermore, the concrete efforts — those easily measured (parent tutors and allocated time increases) — were the most successfully implemented. Thus, there was a pattern of increased direction, and the increased direction was judged to be successful.

Direct Instruction Follow Through implementation

The next report picks up where the SIP (McCarthy et al., 1982) study ends. This research comes from interviews with instructional staff implementing Direct Instruction Follow Through.

Background. In 1978, the University of Oregon Direct Instruction Follow Through Model agreed to sponsor a previously self-sponsored Follow Through site. (See Becker, 1977; Meyer, 1983; Meyer, Gersten, & Gutkin, 1983; or Rhine, 1981, for descriptions of the federally funded Follow Through Project.) The university received funding from the federal government to study the implementation of the Direct Instruction Model. The plan included the assignment of a project manager from the University of Oregon. The manager was responsible for the overall transmission of the model from the sponsor to the site and was the expert in charge of directing instructional changes at the local level. She spent about half her time on site working directly with teachers or teacher aides in their classrooms, observing or demonstrating the various instructional programs. She also trained local principals and worked with a consultant from the university to train three local resource teachers to teach Direct Instruction programs and to supervise the teaching staff in her absence.

The resource teachers were released from teaching responsibilities to become full time supervisors in the Follow Through program. In Fall 1978, when they began working with the project manager and consultant to implement the program, all resource and classroom teachers were new to Direct Instruction Follow Through.

After a week of training with the project manager and consultant, the resource teachers became members of the team that conducted preservice training for all Follow Through teachers and paraprofessional aides before school began. The team also worked together on regularly scheduled inservice training programs for Cohort 1 teachers, limited first year teachers, and classroom aides. Similar preservice and inservice plans were followed in 1979 for Cohort 2 teachers and aides.

An implementation study was conducted to answer three questions: What influence does a new program being implemented have on members of the local education agency? How does a local education agency react to being directed to change? Do a local education agency's views about directed development change as an implementation progresses from the first through the second year? Data were gathered during the second year of the implementation study.

It is important to recall that the federal government forced this site to change curricula. Although negotiations between the federal government, the school district, and the University of Oregon spanned the summer of 1978, the teaching staff first learned of these changes when they returned to school that fall.

The interviews. After assuring all participants that their responses would be reported anonymously, the interviewer reviewed the goals of the program. The individual, semistructured interviews averaged about 75 minutes for teachers and between 30 and 45 minutes for classroom aides. Interviews with teachers focused on personal demographic information: how well the teacher's educational ideology matched the ideology of the Direct Instruction Model; how the teacher perceived the model; how much the teacher had to change to implement the model; how the teacher felt his or her self-concept changed while implementing the model; how adequate the teacher felt the initial training to implement the model had been, including support received during the implementation; and how much support the teacher had received from the principal.

Interviews with classroom aides focused on personal demographics: perceived clarity and difficulty of the model; general attitudes toward the model; perceived adequacy of preservice and inservice training; feelings about the position and responsibilities of a classroom aide; changes aides had made in the program; and perceptions of the impact of the model.

Findings. Results are reported for Cohort 1 teachers and aides who taught Direct Instruction Follow Through in kindergarten or first grade in 1978, limited first year experience staff who received training but no followup, and Cohort 2 aides and teachers who began the Direct Instruction model during the second year of the program's implementation.

Cohort 1 teachers. Seventy-one percent of the Cohort 1 teachers were unclear about implementing the program immediately after preservice training. They developed clearcut ideas of what to do a few months later. Thirty percent found Direct Instruction Follow Through very different from their previous experience because of the emphasis on time on task and the highly structured lessons. Virtually all Cohort 1 teachers found the program easy to master, concise, well defined, and straightforward. Half also found the program nonthreatening.

Cohort 1 teachers often cited problems in their first year due to insensitive monitors, insensitive peers, or inconsistent feedback, although they acknowledged the availability and promptness of materials. They also felt strongly that the program's ambience improved greatly in their second year, although they voiced concerns about placing and teaching new students, holding back higher performing students, and the need for a transition room for incoming students.

They agreed with Direct Instruction Follow Through's emphasis on basic skills and reaffirmed the desire to salvage Follow Through. Half the teachers emphasized the need for Distar, though some complained about the lack of fun.

Cohort 1 teachers generally felt they functioned autonomously in their roles, without support from their peers. Many felt Distar either contributed to their successes or increased their effectiveness. They also said their students increased in self-reliance, social maturity, and overall behavior.

The teachers viewed their preservice and inservice training differently, and their views about preservice changed markedly from their first year to their second. During their first preservice, teachers often felt patronized, rushed, overwhelmed, anxious, and pressured. They described their second preservice as more sensitive, less rushed, and repetitive.

Inservice training varied in relevance and utility, but almost all Cohort 1 teachers maintained that it addressed practical issues. All teachers wanted inservice training to extend beyond a review of teaching techniques.

Teachers painted complicated pictures of the consultants and resource teachers. Half of the teachers felt the project manager's visits were helpful, and three fourths of them said positive things about their project manager, particularly with regard to the manager's feedback to them. A common theme, though, was that teachers wanted more demonstrations and fewer observations from all support staff.

Limited first year teachers. There are predictable similarities and differences between Cohort 1 and limited first year teachers since these groups experienced the same preservice training. They had very different implementation experiences. The limited first year teachers were not expected to have full Direct Instruction implementations. Therefore, they received few services from the project manager, consultants, and resource teachers.

About half the limited first year teachers had only vague ideas of what to do after preservice training. Their comments about the difficulty and magnitude of change expected of them matched comments from Cohort 1 teachers.

Limited first year teachers and Cohort 1 teachers agreed about placement problems caused by incoming students and about Direct Instruction objectives, perceived administrative support, lack of collegial support, and shift in educational ideology from a holistic philosophy to a Direct Instruction philosophy during their two years of Direct Instruction Follow Through experience. Both groups agreed that Distar contributed to their success; 50 percent felt Distar increased their effectiveness.

Cohort 2 teachers. Cohort 2 teachers differed substantially from the Cohort 1 and limited first year teachers, and most of these differences were in a positive direction. A majority of the Cohort 2 teachers were clear about what they were to do immediately after preservice training. They remained clear about their responsibilities throughout the implementation, despite reporting similar difficulties with the magnitude of change required of them that Cohort 1 and limited first year teachers reported.

Half the Cohort 2 teachers felt "checked up on" when they were observed. They also perceived inconsistent feedback and experienced classroom management problems to a slightly greater degree than Cohort 1 and limited first year teachers. Cohort 2 teachers agreed with the other groups about the Direct Instruction objectives, the need to salvage the Follow Through program, and the administrative support they received for their work.

These teachers failed to experience the holistic Direct Instruction clash described by Cohort 1 and limited first year teachers. They did feel, however, that Distar was excessively oriented toward basic skills, and they yearned to "round out" the school day.

Summary of teachers' perspective. Teachers' responses show a progressive pattern of implementation improvement and satisfaction. Generally, the program's rocky start was explained as being caused by pressure on the district to salvage Follow Through. There were substantially more positive comments about the second year's preservice training by the Cohort 1 and limited first year teachers, thus suggesting less confusion and more acceptance of the program by teachers after just one year. All teachers described their difficulties with the magnitude of change required of them, which is not surprising given that most of them had to implement procedures at odds with their previous ideologies. The teachers were happy with plentiful materials and agreed with the Direct Instruction objectives.

Cohort 2 teachers felt they benefited from the support of their peers; of course, they were the first group to have peers who had been through similar implementation experiences. They did not have the same philosophical clash of their own ideologies and the ideologies of the Oregon model. This ready acceptance of the model suggests that things were easier and smoother for the second group of teachers. The level of support for the project manager and resource teachers also suggests that the Cohort 2 teachers appreciated concrete help, particularly help they got in their classrooms.

Classroom aides' interviews. There is much less information from the interviews with the classroom aides. There are, however, several themes from the aides that are similar to comments made by the teachers.

Aides who had had experience teaching Distar prior to the implementation of Direct Instruction Follow Through expressed clearly different perspectives from those of the other aides about their work, although they agreed that Distar was effective and training was repetitive. Cohort 1 aides who were new to Direct Instruction at the beginning of preservice training were pleased with and gratified by their own work. These aides were concerned about their responsibilities and the inconsistent feedback they received. Their responses about observations and demonstrations matched teachers' responses: They wanted more demonstrations and fewer observations.

The limited first year aides split. Half found inservice training boring and half found it helpful. They described the Distar program as clear and straightforward and described their work as a challenge. They were impressed with their students' performance and recognized the importance of strengthening the Follow Through program.

Cohort 2 classroom aides were almost unanimous in finding Distar easy to learn. They credited their previous preservice and inservice training with helping them and viewed the resource teachers as sensitive and supportive. These aides also felt the resource teachers' classroom visits were crucial.

Most of the aides' comments were similar to the Follow Through teachers' comments. Generally, they viewed help they received positively, though, like the teachers, they would have preferred more demonstrations and fewer observations.

Discussion, implications, and advice to administrators

This chapter began by tracing research on program implementation from the findings of the frequently cited Rand Report (Berman & McLaughlin, 1975) to the results of the Experience Based Career Education program's attempts to implement the Rand Report's concept of mutual adaptation (Farrar et al., 1980a, 1980b), and then to the reanalysis of the Rand Report data (Datta, 1980, 1981) on program implementation. By tracing mutual adaptation from its derivation to attempted uses and reanalyses, it is apparent that there are serious problems with its roots and with its outcomes. Furthermore, the SIP strategies became increasingly directive as the program progressed, and the Follow Through study, which was clearly directed development from the beginning, showed teaching staff acceptance after two years. A rather clear profile of expert help emerges from these studies. The expert who made the implementation work was typically one who worked closely with staff in classrooms.

These findings on change efforts complement a line of studies on teacher use of new techniques. Joyce (1981) found that when teachers attended only workshops on new techniques, they achieved an implementation level of about 15 percent—they incorporated little information from the workshop into their classroom practices. Joyce reported increasing levels of implementation as the help moved into their classrooms; teachers receiving practical expert help in their classrooms implemented about 85 percent of the new practices. Such different results from these treatments are not at all surprising if we consider what we expect teachers to do when implementing new strategies. First, we expect them to change behaviors. Even simple behavioral changes are difficult to achieve. When we ask or demand that teachers change how they teach, particularly when new techniques are different ideologically and behaviorally from those they learned and accepted in college, we are asking for what Kuhn (1970) called a paradigm shift. Changes of this magnitude are difficult to accomplish, but they can be expected if teachers have adequate feedback and support while they are learning new things.

In summary, what do we know about how to change public schools? What should we say to the superintendent who wants more students in the district to read at or above grade level? Contrary to popular practice, research suggests that superintendents should decide what they want changed and how they want to make the change. They need to recognize that regardless of the opinions and ideas people have, their chances of bringing about change probably hinge on whether there is some directed development. After superintendents make their choices, they should enlist experts to work with the teaching staff. The experts need to work in the classroom in a pragmatic way with groups chosen by the superintendent. These experts need to be proficient enough to model for teachers and to observe carefully, because it is a blend of demonstrations, observations, and guided practice that is most likely to bring about changes for teaching.

References

Anderson, L.M., Evertson, C.M., and Brophy, J.E. An experimental study of effective teaching in first-grade reading groups. *Elementary School Journal,* 1979, *79,* 193-322.

Becker, W.C. Teaching reading and language to the disadvantaged—what we have learned from field research. *Harvard Educational Review,* 1977, *47,* 518-543.

Berman, P., and McLaughlin, M. Federal programs supporting educational change, volume 4: *The findings in review.* Santa Monica, CA: Rand Corporation, 1975.

Datta, L.E. Changing times: The study of federal programs supporting educational change and the case for local problem solving. *Teachers College Record,* 1980, *82,* 101-115.

Datta, L.E. Damn the experts and full steam ahead. *Evaluation Review,* 1981, *5,* 5-31.

Edmonds, R. Effective schools for the urban poor. *Educational Leadership,* 1979, *16,* 1-16.

Farrar, E., DeSanctis, J.E., and Cohen, D.K. Views from below: Implementation research in education. *Teachers College Record,* 1980a, *82,* 77-100.

Farrar, E., DeSanctis, J.E., and Cohen, D.K. The lawn party: The evolution of federal programs in local settings. *Phi Delta Kappan,* 1980b, *82,* 167-171.

Good, T., and Grouws, D. The Missouri mathematics effectiveness project. *Journal of Educational Psychology,* 1979, *71,* 355-362.

Goodlad, J.I. *The dynamics of educational change.* New York: McGraw-Hill, 1975.

Havelock, R.G. *The change agent's guide to innovation in education.* Englewood Cliffs, NJ: Educational Technology Publications, 1973.

Joyce, B. *Guaranteeing carryover from workshops to classrooms.* Invited address, University of Oregon, 1981.

Kennedy, M. Findings from the follow through planned variation study. *Educational Researcher,* 1978, *7,* 3-11.

Kuhn, T.S. *The structure of scientific revolutions.* Chicago: University of Chicago Press, 1970.

McCarthy, D.P., Canner, J., Chawla, L., and Pershing, A. *School improvement project: Third annual process evaluation, 1981-1982.* New York: New York Public Schools, 1982.

Meyer, L.A. Teaching basic skills to low income children: One community's approach. *Journal of Rural Education,* Spring 1983.

Meyer, L.A., Gersten, R.M., and Gutkin, J. Direct instruction: A project follow through success story. *Elementary School Journal,* 1983, *84,* 241-252.

Rhine, W.R. (Ed.). *Making schools more effective.* New York: Academic Press, 1981.

Rivlin, A.M., and Timpane, P.M. (Eds.). *Planned variations in education.* Washington, DC: Brookings, 1975.

Schmuck, R.A., Runkel, P.J., Arends, J.H., and Arends, R.I. *The second handbook of organization development in schools.* Palo Alto, CA: Mayfield, 1977.

Stallings, J. Allocated academic learning time revisited, or beyond time on task. *Educational Researcher,* 1980, *9,* 11-16.

Weick, K.E. Educational organizations as loosely coupled systems. *Administrative Science Quarterly,* 1976, *21,* 1-19.

Weikart, D.P., and Banet, B.A. Model design problems in follow through. In A.M. Rivlin and P.M. Timpane (Eds.), *Planned variations in education.* Washington, DC: Brookings, 1975.

Zimiles, H., Mayer, R., and Wickens, E. *Bringing child-centered education to the public schools: A study of school intervention.* New York: Bank Street College of Education, 1980.

Zoref, L.S. *A prototype for how to evaluate implementation of a structured educational program.* Unpublished doctoral dissertation, University of Oregon, 1981.

Prelude

*I*f Chapter 3 tells us why we should adopt a directed development model of change, then Chapter 4, after providing us with a broader context, tells us how. Carnine begins with an insightful analysis of why innovations fail, outlining four obstacles to change and a variety of factors that permit those obstacles to operate. Then he turns to the issue of what you have to worry about if you are going to "do it right." He gives us three metaphors for being a change agent (the detective, the hero, and the manager) and discusses the components and stages in effective attempts to introduce change. This chapter is full of information, and it should be read twice, once for gist and once for detail, before it assumes its rightful role as a valuable reference tool.

4

Douglas Carnine

How to overcome barriers
to student achievement

U ntil recently the prognosis has been bleak for increasing the
academic achievement of at risk students. Early sociological
data (Coleman et al., 1966; Jencks et al., 1972) have been used to
support the belief that schooling makes little difference, though
more recently even Jencks (1979) seems to attribute more importance to the schooling process. In the past several years an empirical
knowledge base about effective classroom practices (Denham &
Lieberman, 1980) and school level activities (Clark, Lotto, & Mc-
Carthy, 1980) has become available, creating a glimmer of opti-
mism. An integration of current classroom research yields a
somewhat old fashioned description of effective teaching (Stevens &
Rosenshine, 1981). In classrooms where children are making serious academic gains, teachers spend much of the day on instruction
in academic areas. The teacher demonstrates in a clear, precise fashion how to handle new types of problems before giving students
practice on the material. Students often work in small groups, receiving continual feedback from the teacher on the accuracy of their
performance. Teachers ensure that the material is not too difficult or
too easy; in fact, an optimal success level seems to be 80 to 90 percent (Stevens & Rosenshine).

The effective teaching methods identified by Stevens and
Rosenshine do not imply cold, unfeeling teachers or robot like students; the opposite is often true. In ethnographic studies it has been
found that effective teachers tend to be warm and concerned

This research was supported in part by the National Institute of Education. The views expressed do not represent those of the NIE.

(Tikunoff, Berliner, & Rist, 1975). Similarly, students in classrooms of these teachers are observed to be convivial, cooperative, and supportive. Effective teachers have high expectations for their students and are skilled enough to realize their expectations.

Stevens and Rosenshine cited studies that looked at classrooms. Other researchers have taken a different approach—identifying those low income schools that are effective and delineating the critical components that characterize these schools (Edmonds, 1979). A *Phi Delta Kappan* analysis of over 1,200 studies affirmed the existence of a rather extensive knowledge base, "now rather precisely defined—[that] can ensure school success in the urban setting" (Clark, Lotto, & McCarthy, 1980).

A close look at Clark, Lotto, and McCarthy's findings on school effectiveness research discloses variables that touch the very core of education.

> The leader's attitude toward urban education and expectations for school or program success determines the impact of the leader on exceptional schools.

> The greater the specificity or focus of the training program in terms of goals or processes, the greater the likelihood of its success.

> Reductions in adult/child ratios are associated with positive school performance.

> Successful schools and programs are characterized by clearly stated curricular goals and objectives.

Their findings imply that improving instruction in urban elementary schools would require new behavior and attitudes on the part of principals and down to earth staff training programs that meet teachers' and students' immediate needs. These and other needed changes would have to be massive and sustained—not one day workshops or brief "add on" activities that last a few weeks.

As educational policymakers become aware of the magnitude and quantity of changes needed to increase student achievement,

Carnine

they are directing greater attention to the change process (Berman & McLaughlin, 1978; Fullan & Pomfret, 1977; Hall & Loucks, 1977; Herriot & Gross, 1979; Sarason, 1971; Stallings, 1975). For example, the director of the National Association of Educational Progress said, "Where we can go in our quest to improve educational performance requires careful, sophisticated, and deliberate planning" (Forbes, 1981, p. 332). This point has been made often in the past; what is new is the growing awareness that the implementation of the plan must be sophisticated and deliberate. The difficulty in the implementation of such plans stems from the profound complexity of the obstacles. An NIE official attributed this complexity to

> [d]isorder inherent in conflicting governmental policy, the inconsistent positions and demands of a variety of special interests, and a prevailing school and community climate that is inconsistent with, and uncongenial to, the requirements of learning (Tomlinson, 1981).

Several approaches have been taken to support change in school practices: (1) development of innovations designed to meet particular needs and their subsequent dissemination to schools; (2) technical assistance in identifying problems, finding solutions, and managing changes; and (3) provision of general school support in cases where systematic change efforts are assumed to be fruitless (Datta, 1980). Regardless of the approach taken, attempts to understand and guide change usually come in the form of a model. One of the better ones, the Educational Leadership Obstacle Course Model developed by Herriott and Gross (1979), describes five stages in the change process. While the model seems conceptually sound, its weaknesses include too great a reliance on analysis of the dimensions of leadership and too general an approach for use in specific school situations. By their own admission, the model "offers no detailed specifications about the specific obstacles likely to arise when a major innovation is introduced..." (p. 362).

The first part of this chapter focuses on those specific obstacles that impede the implementation and institutionalization of effective, well defined, large scale innovations. (To qualify as effective, an innovation should have consistent results across time and across settings. Such evidence, which is extremely important, is impossible to obtain unless the innovation is well enough defined to be installed and maintained in various communities.)

Obstacles can arise regardless of the type of change or of the approach taken to support the change. Without an understanding of potential barriers to improving the education of at risk students, change efforts will continue to be ineffectual and short lived. This point is all too often overlooked and discounted, or as March (1978) noted,

> Crises in education, as in other domains, characteristically appear more profound in the enthusiasms of contemporaries than they do in retrospect. Indeed, we know that glorification of problems is an investment in the triumphs of their solution.

The following discussion of barriers and their causes may suffer from March's enthusiasms. However, the reality for millions of school failures is harsh (Ozenne et al., 1974; Wolf, 1978).

Barriers to educational change

> The major studies of curriculum reform have shown that where training, the introduction of materials, vertical political solidarity and staff and administrative commitment are brought together, there is considerable movement. Gradually, the school returns to the normative patterns which characterize most American schools and the innovations lose their steam. The problem is a worldwide one (Hersh et al., 1981).

Even though teachers' greatest rewards have to do with serving their students (Dunn, 1980), innovative practices that help teachers better serve students are often underused or misused. This happens in four ways: through discrediting, delaying, distorting, and, ultimately, discontinuing.

Discrediting

If an innovation is discredited, pressures to adopt it are minimal. Innovations are usually discredited through intellectual or quasiintellectual activities such as attributing their success to unique factors not found in other settings; objecting to the values represented by the innovation; questioning, criticizing, and ignoring any evaluation that judges the innovation to be effective; or even claiming that the innovative practice has already been incorporated into current practices.

According to the uniqueness argument, the effective instructional program that operated for over a decade at P.S. 137 in the Ocean Hill Brownsville section of New York could not work in P.S. 73, which is located only three blocks away—despite the fact that the program in P.S. 137 operated effectively for twelve years with five different principals, four different compensatory education directors, and more than fifty different teachers. If this view is true, scientific work in education is a contradiction in terms, since, to be valid, scientific knowledge must be true in more than one setting. What would be the reaction to a doctor who said that heart surgery could be done successfully on Fourteenth Street in Chicago but not on Eleventh Street? In education, people readily accept data showing that in one urban school most students can read while in another school a few blocks away most students cannot read without ever considering that this may be due to differences in the specific instructional processes going on in the two buildings.

Undermining an innovation by questioning the values it represents is more subtle. "For the educationists, the doctrine of the whole child is the magical balm that washes away their sins. Ask a question about skills, and you get T.S. Eliot, transforming the question to one about values" (Lyons, 1980). One program, validated as exemplary in twelve states by the Department of Education's Joint Dissemination Review Panel, was seemingly discredited in a PBS documentary by a survey of principals who said that the program does not address creativity and other aspects of the whole child. While the program's effectiveness was well known, it was believed to be insufficiently humanistic, turning teachers and children into robots. One principal, new to a building, forbade two teachers to continue the program even though he had never seen it in use; he even refused to observe the teachers using it.

Similarly, critics can claim that evaluations of an innovative program are not valid because they fail to measure what is truly important. As Anderson and his colleagues state, "Any program that wishes to rid itself forever of the discomforts of evaluation need only add to its list of objectives one metaphysical, obscure, or otherwise unmeasurable purpose..." (Anderson et al., 1978). It is unreasonable to reject an evaluation because it did not measure what may be impossible to measure (e.g., the inner feelings, aspirations, or creative potential of a generation of school children). Nonetheless, an unpopular evaluation finding can be discounted by emphasizing what was not measured.

Another way of discrediting a successful innovation, one that may seem almost inconceivable to the naive reader, is simply to ignore its success. "Although pupil achievement data are routinely collected for individual students and are used to monitor their progress and determine their opportunities, the same data are rarely aggregated so as to provide a basis for assessing the performance of individual teachers, schools, or districts" (Meyer, Scott, & Deal, 1979). By failing to aggregate data and compare progress across schools and classrooms, administrators relieve themselves of the responsibility to provide remedies to low performing schools or to explain why some schools are effective.

Delaying

Even if an innovation is not discredited, its adoption can be delayed. While delaying is characteristic of many fields, there are some exceptions. In medicine, technological advances often are accepted rapidly. In one study, a new drug was adopted by 90 percent of the physicians in four communities within seventeen months. Typically, the widespread adoption of an educational innovation is at least ten times slower (Carlson, 1964).

Distorting

No innovation is implementation proof. Innovations that are not discredited and delayed still can turn out to be ineffectual as a result of extensive modifications. For an untried innovation, a process of adaption seems reasonable; in fact, all things being equal, the more an innovation is adapted, the more likely its acceptance in a school (Berman & McLaughlin, 1975). Too often, adaptation becomes a euphemism for distortion. For example, Centra and Porter (1980) cited several studies of team teaching in which the investigators couldn't even identify which teachers were working in teams. The innovation had been transformed in such a way that team teaching no longer differed from traditional practice. Another common occurrence is selecting only a part of the innovation for implementation (in the name of eclecticism) and then attributing the subsequent failure to the entire innovation. Finally, an innovative practice adopted by a district may be implemented in name only, characterized by Charters and Jones (1973) as a nonevent.

Sometimes distortion seems like sabotage. For example, one small urban school adopted an innovative program that required paraprofessionals and specific instructional materials. One year the central administration waited until Thanksgiving to hire paraprofessionals, even though trained people and funds were available; over 3,200 hours of instructional time were lost. A few years earlier, the same district ignored an order for essential instructional material for over six months, resulting in the loss of thousands of hours of instruction. Disruptions also can be effected by transferring key personnel to other schools or bringing in personnel opposed to the innovation.

Discontinuing

Even those innovative practices that are eventually implemented and proven to be quite effective often are discontinued. Rowan (1977) found that innovations that had nothing to do with instruction (e.g., school health and cafeteria services) had the greatest likelihood of survival. Those indirectly related to instruction (guidance counseling and psychological testing services) had a moderate likelihood of survival. Innovations that actually dealt with instruction were the least stable and were terminated most quickly.

Abandonment of a program by administrators can occur in the face of public support. At a school board meeting for a small rural community, several parents testified in support of a relatively new, highly structured compensatory education program. One parent's three oldest children, who started school before the district installed the new program, hadn't learned to read. Later, two younger children, who had the benefit of the new program, tutored their older siblings. The parent was worried that her sixth child, only four years old, would be a school failure if the program were dropped. Despite the district's acknowledgement that the program was quite effective with at risk children, the board voted to discontinue it after teachers charged that the program was too structured and had too narrow a focus.

Contributing factors

"The greatest difficulties lie where we are not looking for them."

Goethe

If discrediting, delaying, distorting, and discontinuing are as prevalent as they seem to be, implications are distressing for disseminating knowledge related to effective schooling. This section discusses several origins of the obstacles to implementing effective school practices. A better understanding of the origins could lead to ideas for overcoming them.

These sources are not tied in any simple way to the barriers discussed earlier. Opposition to an innovation may stem from multiple sources and may appear in efforts to discredit, delay, distort, and discontinue. This opposition usually comes from supporters of a competing goal or method, whether it be the status quo or an alternative innovation.

Conflicts with existing norms and value systems

The pluralism of American society probably precludes a consensus about any particular method or goal in education (Pincus, 1974; White, 1984). While this chapter focuses on increasing the achievement and self esteem of students, many educators have other goals. Some of these goals are primarily noncognitive, for instance, enhancing social development. Other goals do not focus on the students, but on the educators.

Georgious (1973) raises an even more serious concern, that the actual constituents served by schools are the individuals who work in schools. His implication is that schools exist for teachers; state departments for bureaucrats; universities for professors; and central offices for administrators. A similar image is implied in Burlingame's (1978) description of schools as social systems bound together by shared "secrets" about staff, students, the students' families, and what he calls the seasons of the school year—the predictable events revolving around sports, vacations, or instructional topics covered at different times. The resulting climate and expectations often place less emphasis on student achievement than on preserving the traditional roles of the educators.

> It is probably true that many attempts at innovation will fail, not for technical reasons, but because the demand is not there—society prefers the status quo (Pincus, 1974).

Even after an innovation is mandated by the central office of a district and produces significant achievement gains in students, conflicts can arise from divergent priorities and expectations. Cronin (1980) interviewed teachers from seven low income minority schools in a large urban school district. Each school was required by the central administration to use a highly structured curriculum. At the end of two years, many teachers favored the program because both they and their students had experienced increased success. But some teachers said they opposed the program because its structured nature conflicted with their belief that the act of teaching should not be constrained by externally created structures, even though they acknowledged the students were learning more than they had ever imagined possible.

A few teachers requested transfers to middle income schools because the program required them to expend considerable energy teaching all the economically disadvantaged students in their classrooms, not just the brighter half of the group. They found this to be work they didn't enjoy. The behaviors of the principals in the seven schools studied by Cronin were considered by virtually all thirty-three teachers to be irrelevant to the implementation of the innovation and to the increased student achievement gains.

Attitudes of teachers and principals are crucial, particularly since about 85 percent of most schools' operating budgets is allocated to personnel. With innovations in education, numerous situations arise each day that generate conflict with teacher norms and typical work behavior. Teachers may find themselves facing difficult questions; for example, "Since academic learning time is so important, should I replace half of the unstructured exploration time with reading instruction? Because of the importance of mastery learning, do I need to work with Johnny an extra five minutes each day until he learns to solve subtraction problems?" These decisions are painful to make because they often involve reallocating teacher time and energy that previously has gone into other, more enjoyable activities. One analysis suggests that "to the extent that the innovation is inconsistent with important norms and practices in the school district, it may, by its very implementation, create the pressures that ultimately lead to its discontinuation" (Gaynor, Barrow, & Klenke, 1980, p. 52).

Loose coupling

Traditional notions or models of school organization and purpose may fail to reflect reality. For example, the principal is assumed to be the instructional leader of the school. However, principals usually are not instructional leaders; they are employers, delegators, information sources, advocates, and resource procurers (Wyant, 1980). Less than 2 percent of principals' time involves instructional leadership (Howell, 1981). Furthermore, teachers do not perceive principals as instructional leaders (Mazzarella, 1977). Many consider as poor the prognosis for principals actually assuming greater responsibility for and interest in school effectiveness issues. "Changing education by changing educational administration is like changing the course of the Mississippi River by spitting into the Allegheny" (March, 1978). For many educators, the conclusion is obvious—principals should not be accountable in any way for schooling as it relates to student achievement: "Take the principal off the hooks marked 'change agent' and 'instructional leader' " (Salley, McPherson, & Baehr, 1975).

According to Meyer, Scott, and Deal (1979, p. 3), schools are not, and never have been, organized around a knowledge base for delivering quality instruction to students.

> It is most crucial for a school, in order to survive, to conform to institutional rules—including community understandings—defining teacher categories and credentials, pupil selection and definition, proper topics of instruction, and appropriate facilities. It is less essential that a school make sure that teaching and learning activities are efficiently coordinated.

One reflection of the relatively low importance attached to efficient coordination of instruction is loose coupling (Weick, 1976). Generally, administrators do not systematically monitor the instructionally relevant behaviors of subordinates. Teachers act independently of principals, just as principals usually act independently of central administrators (Morris et al., 1981). Principals' policy pronouncements about instruction bear no consistent relationship to what happens in classrooms. Classrooms often are characterized as autonomous units, cottage industries, or cellular organizations. According to Lortie (1969), "Indications are that that which is most central and unique to schools—instruction—is least controlled by specific and literally enforced rules and regulations.

According to the informal covenant, teachers agree to implement the innovations suggested by the principal by attending workshops on the innovation. However, principals rarely demand that teachers actually implement the program, virtually never following up or observing classroom practice (Parrish, 1981).

In analyzing the problems of teacher training in Texas, Lyons (1980, p. 109) aptly described the set of attitudes that coexist with loose coupling. The Texas Education Authority

> insists it is powerless to demand competence, due to political pressure exerted on the legislature by the colleges. The

colleges insist they must assume prospective teachers to be literate when they arrive from the high schools. High school teachers say they cannot ignore subject matter in their courses to teach skills that should have been mastered in junior high. Eighth-grade teachers blame seventh-grade teachers, and so forth back to first grade, where teachers have no one left to blame but society, which they do. The National Education Association (NEA), the chief proponent of no-fault teaching, urges us in a pamphlet to take note, before deciding who is responsible for plummeting test scores, of the distractions which characterized American life in the past decade or so. Among the nominees are the war, the draft, riots, corruption in high places, assassinations, and television. The "decade of distraction," we are told, "puts an additional burden on teachers who are asked to provide stability while other aspects of life are in chaos." If everyone is to blame, in other words, no one is to blame.

With loose coupling, systematic planning for introducing and maintaining an innovation becomes essentially impossible. Cohen, March, and Olsen (1972) describe schools as organized anarchies in which one finds "choices looking for problems and issues, feelings looking for decision situations in which they might be aired, solutions looking for issues to which they might be the answer, decision makers looking for work."

The characterization of schools as loosely coupled, organized anarchies conforming to institutional rules contrasts sharply with traditional assumptions that schools are rational and goal oriented with centralized control (Corwin, 1973). While requirements for formal coordination and control may be minimal in some settings, that is not the case for urban schools; loose coupling can be particularly damaging for them.

A middle class, small school, with a placid environment, would require for coordination and control only interpersonal support, reinforcement, and the creation of general informal understandings of how things are done. In contrast, a large, urban, lower class school attempting a new program of individualized instruction in reading would require the administrator to do much more work on formal organization in the area of coordination and control of instruction (Cohen et al., 1977).

As loosely coupled organizations, schools do not operate according to the dictates of control, rational planning, and progress (Wolcott, 1977). That is not to say that loose coupling does not have advantages. Weick (1976) lists several:

1. It allows many independent perceptions and therefore better knowledge of the environment.
2. It permits a greater number of mutations and novel solutions and therefore encourages easier adaptation to a wider range of changes in the environment.
3. If a breakdown or deterioration in one portion of the system can be sealed off, it will not affect other portions.
4. It allows more room for self-determination by the members of the organization, thereby increasing the sense of efficacy for each.
5. It makes administrative functions less expensive because it takes time and money to coordinate people.

The arguments in support of loose coupling may be flawed in two ways. First, although schools as they are currently organized may serve middle and upper middleclass students, they often fail to teach at risk students. To legitimize loose coupling may be tantamount to endorsing an inferior education for at risk students. Second, though alternatives to loose coupling were not possible a few years ago, research now provides viable alternatives. For example, Derr and Deal (1978) characterized schools as numerous, diffuse, unclear, and often with conflicting goals; having no well developed technologies; at the mercy of the environment; showing a lack of professionalism; and with little interdependence among staff. Organizations with these characteristics, so the argument goes, are aptly suited for loose coupling. However, the research cited at the beginning of this chapter, which relates student achievement to school and classroom contexts, suggests that the characteristics identified by Derr and Deal are not pandemic. A consensus is possible, at least concerning the importance of basic skills; an extensive technology exists; schools can become beacons of excellence for the community; and professional cooperation in inservice is possible.

Limited knowledge

A convergence of knowledge about school effectiveness has occurred within the past few years. The newness of this knowledge, combined with practitioners' cynicism toward research findings, may account for some of the resistance to adopting practices shown to relate to improved achievement.

> A reason often given for the absence of bureaucratic controls on instruction is the lack of a rational body of pedagogical knowledge. If teaching is essentially an intuitive and unknowable activity, then there is no way to control teaching acts through monitoring of either the methods used or the outcomes achieved (Cohen, 1978, p. 8).

Desire to minimize stress

Conforming to the numerous, often conflicting institutional rules that face educators—technological, legal, political, economic, demographic, ecological, and cultural—produces stress (Duke, 1979). To reduce stress, educators channel reform into safer areas, "those that involve spending more money on the existing resource mix...or those that involve the kinds of changes in curriculum or administration that don't seem to threaten organized groups in or out of the bureaucracy" (Pincus, 1974, p. 124). Educators also attempt to minimize the number of institutional rules to which they must conform. If Meyer and others are correct in asserting that the application of knowledge about school effectiveness has never been an institutional practice, educators could be expected to avoid the institutionalization of effective instructional techniques. "Efforts to actually inspect educational outputs, to coordinate the specifics of what is taught to individual students by particular teachers would invariably increase conflicts with parents and students, cause dissatisfaction among teachers, and vastly increase the burdens of administrators" (Meyer, Scott, & Deal, 1979).

Even though avoiding responsibility for providing instructional solutions to student failure reduces strain, educators cannot blatantly ignore the public's expectations. Current moves require that schools at least resemble rational, responsible organizations. For example, Burlingame (1978, p. 21) noted that alleged innovations, such as Planning Programing Budgeting Systems (PPBS) or Management by Objective (MBO) are often adopted to "make school management appear rational to the public. Teachers view these innovations as devices for postponing decisions or legitimizing decisions that have already been made."

Lack of competition for clients

As monopolies, schools do not compete with other organizations for clients; thus, many incentives for improving services are missing. "There is no struggle for survival for this organization. Like the domesticated animal, these organizations are fed and cared for. Existence is guaranteed" (Carlson, 1964, p. 266). The monopolistic nature of public education allows schools "to render what they term adequate service to only some of their clients" (Carlson, 1964, p. 168). Ogbu (1978) found that schools are expected to educate middleclass whites, but not blacks, for leadership roles.

Conservative publishers

Publishers do not readily incorporate knowledge about effective instructional practices into their textbooks for fear of creating an unusual and unsuccessful product that might reduce their share of a multimillion dollar market. Elementary grade texts are often written by editors with no teacher training or experience. In fact, according to a marketing survey by one publisher, teaching experience may not be a requisite for a successful textbook author. This publisher found that the single most important determinant in districts' purchase of a basal series was the attractiveness of the art work, hardly a variable of instructional effectiveness in the curriculum.

When concerns about the effectiveness of texts are raised, publishers are reluctant to respond. Two decades ago, Chall (1967) reviewed commonly used basal reading programs, reporting several serious flaws relating to instruction in decoding. Revisions made in response to these analyses have been largely superficial. Phonics exercises have been added as an afterthought, but have not resulted in major changes in student readers.

Dysfunctional research

Gilbert (1978) found that researchers usually wrote for other researchers, investigating variables that schools could not change (such as teacher personality traits or family background characteristics), developing theories that lacked practical application (such as the relationship between neurological development and reading instruction), or merely describing current practice. Practitioners have become cynical, and the cynicism is well founded (Phillips, 1980).

> Many of the innovations adopted by the schools are not innovations at all, but only fads, since there is little or no serious attempt to validate them in terms of productivity or effectiveness criteria, nor is there any market-like mechanism which automatically separates wheat from chaff. The validation process for educational innovation is ultimately measured by bureaucratic and social acceptability (Pincus, 1974, p. 119).

Educational researchers frequently have adopted models from the physical sciences, characterized by elaborate theories and laboratory research. In the physical sciences, findings are generalizable because the essential properties of matter are basically the same inside and outside the laboratory. In contrast, the context and nature of learning tasks are not the same inside and outside the laboratory and are not the same for skilled and unskilled learners. Consequently, much theory building and research based on contrived experiments using college sophomores have been irrelevant to instruction. Similarly, research that never goes beyond descriptions of pressing problems does not fill the need for knowledge on how to

Carnine

improve management and instructional practices. Such knowledge must have ecological validity, which means that the research context must closely resemble the context in which the practice takes place (Snow, 1974).

The direction of some research efforts has changed over the past several years. Many findings, though mostly based on correlations, now provide concrete suggestions for improving instruction, especially in elementary schools with economically disadvantaged students. However, because of lingering or generalized cynicism on the part of practitioners, these research findings have had little effect on education.

Unresponsive colleges, schools, and departments of education

Since colleges are responsible for preparing teachers, they might seem the ideal vehicle for introducing school improvement innovations. This does not seem to be the case. Professors who are former public school teachers are quite familiar with institutional rules, the nature of basal textbooks, the irrelevance of school effectiveness research, and the triviality of basic skills.

Something is certainly askew in teacher training, even in the public's view. The article that won the National Magazine Award for public service noted, "Teacher education is a massive fraud. It drives out dedicated people, rewards incompetence, and wastes millions of dollars" (Lyons, 1980, p. 108). The same article reported that half of the 535 first year teachers in Dallas recently failed a skills test that was passed by most of the junior high students in a private Dallas school. Even students of education do not seem to regard teacher training programs very positively. Dornbush and Scott (1975) found that elementary school teachers felt their preparation did not help them teach effectively. In contrast, nurses regarded their professional training as important.

State and federal policies

Since education is primarily the responsibility of local districts, state and federal officials are reluctant to advocate anything other than prevalent practice. For example, in some states, state department officials review and adopt textbooks for statewide use. The criteria for selection of textbooks reflect the shared backgrounds of educators. In Oregon, an innovative mathematics program that had been empirically proven to be effective in teaching basic and cognitive skills was rejected because it did not conform to traditional rules about what a textbook should "look like." The controversy was ultimately resolved in court. In part, the case determined whether the criterion of effectiveness is at least as important as conformity to common practice—it is not.

Similar conclusions could be drawn about the activities of federal officials. They are concerned about the presence of proper documents, how funds are spent, or the racial composition of schools, but rarely are they concerned about issues of educational effectiveness. Often, the plethora of federal requirements actually hinders effective instruction.

Uninterested professional groups

Though unions have clarified the teacher's role (Burlingame, 1978) and promoted the financial welfare of teachers, they have done little to increase educators' interest in new knowledge about instruction. It is unlikely that unions will support innovations that might disrupt the autonomy of teachers or threaten teachers with seniority. Similarly, other professional associations (e.g., the National Council of Teachers of English) only recently have made school effectiveness issues a priority.

An uninformed public

Parents and the school boards who represent them may seem the most likely groups to demand the implementation of effective innovations. Sadly, this is seldom the case. Parents are often intimidated by educational research, as well as jargon, or are told that practices do not exist that would work with their children. They are told that the root of school failure lies with the child, the parents, or society at large, but not with the school. A court appointed team evaluated the quality of education in over twenty minority schools in a large urban district. They reported that principals blamed poor academic achievement on factors such as lack of parental interest, pupils' lack of intrinsic motivation, home background, and poverty

Carnine

(Cronin & Peterson, 1980). Ryan (1971) called this phenomenon "blaming the victim."

In all likelihood, parents and school boards will not serve as advocates for effective change until they become informed about what can work. Tucker and Ziegler (1980) reported that only 7 percent of the statements made at the school board meetings in eleven selected districts dealt with curriculum. This situation can change. School boards could informally assess the instructional orientation of the districts' administration by questioning administrators. With the information gained from the answers, board members could request a school improvement plan.

Implications

On one level, a constructive stance toward the contributing factors is easy.

1. Establish awareness about schooling priorities.
2. Tighten school management.
3. Increase knowledge about effective schooling practices.
4. Create new professional norms that support learning new skills.
5. Increase competition in schooling via vouchers or other means.
6. Use market pressure and persuasion to entice publishers to incorporate new knowledge about effective practices.
7. Support research that will inform practitioners.
8. Carry out extensive inservice training programs in colleges of education.
9. Tie some government funding and regulations to quality of instruction.
10. Make professional groups serious advocates for improved professional performance.
11. Educate the public about the attributes of effective schools.

These prescriptions have several shortcomings. The most pronounced is contained in the adage "easier said than done." Even in today's environment, with greater interest in education than at any time since Sputnik, few of the eleven prescriptions are receiving anything more than token attention. Current thinking is at the level of giving teachers competency tests and making high school students take another year of mathematics. Getting beyond these easy to mandate requirements is difficult and not seen as necessary. The final section of this chapter is intended for those educators who feel differently, who are convinced that school improvement cannot be brought about by legislatures, commissions, or committees.

The change agent

Introducing new practices is quite different from maintaining the status quo. The role of change agent evokes images like politician, energizer, and manager. These are familiar images for administrators. Less common images of the educational change agent — for example, a detective or a hero — are also quite important. The hero champions the innovation, though not like the prince who slays a dragon, finds a magic potion, or rescues a maiden. Some notion of heroism is probably required, though, if change agents are to persevere and be courageous in the face of those who would discredit, delay, distort, and discontinue an innovation. A conventional approach to change involves policy, persuasion, and preference. Administrators can easily set a new policy, try to persuade some teachers to follow it, and leave the implementation to teacher preference, but significant change seldom results from this sequence.

An approach calling for assertion, agitation, and action is needed for serious change. Tenacity is needed to monitor this change process. Championing innovations to improve achievement requires keeping track of unobtrusive information based on the components of the innovation, such as content covered, success rate of students, and status of staff development efforts. The tenacious manager consistently checks to make sure information on implementation is being gathered, analyzed, acted upon, and later checked. In other words, breakdowns in the change process are identified while there is still time for corrective action. A leader needs to start out by asserting, agitating, and ensuring action, and continue by being tenacious in checking and following up.

Carnine

The detective ferrets out information about the feelings and abilities needed for an innovation to succeed. Innovations designed to improve student academic achievement assume a certain level of commitment to achievement. Verifying that assumption requires serious attempts to examine the degree to which a school faculty truly values student achievement in relation to other goals. Nurturing and protecting a major innovation necessitate extra work for teachers and administrators who may be unwilling to admit their indifference or opposition to the innovation.

Asking faculty members about the value of student achievement may not be very revealing, yielding answers expressed in terms of espoused goals (Argyris & Schon, 1974). A more revealing procedure is to identify the actual rewards and sanctions, both formal and informal, that operate in a school. If instructional practices are largely neglected, a change effort that targets academics will require brilliant planning, skilled execution, and heroic devotion.

As important as assessing commitment is comparing current practices with ideal practices, as represented by the yet to be installed innovation. For present purposes, the assessment would focus on components relevant to effective instruction: appropriate difficulty level of curricular material, staff available to provide instructional time (resource personnel and paraprofessionals, either paid or volunteer), proficiency of staff in specific teaching skills, allocation of time to instruction, classroom organization, presence of a system for periodic monitoring of student learning (mastery level and amount of content covered), and a quality control system for keeping track of the factors (Carnine & Silbert, 1979). Extreme discrepancies between the actual and ideal for any of these components pose problems for the implementation of a major innovation.

Thus the detective may find two types of problems—those related to values or beliefs and those related to skills and knowledge. Often both types of problems occur together. For example, first grade teachers who have difficulty applying mastery learning techniques during small group instruction may require extensive technical assistance in the classroom to deal with their skill deficiency. However, intensive classroom supervision violates the informal covenant, assumptions of loose coupling, and teacher norms of professionalism.

The change process

> In developing a 6-hour training course for Korean War soldiers on how to avoid trenchfoot and frostbite, greater sources of casualties than gunshot wounds, I soon saw that something was wrong. The entire subject matter could be stated in a single sentence: "Keep Your Socks Dry!" The course was a mistake, but it did open a portal to discovery. For the first time I saw the difference between deficiencies of knowledge and deficiencies of execution. Even after watching movies of toes falling off, soldiers simply wouldn't go to the trouble to keep their socks dry (Gilbert, 1978).

Change agents both move and are moved within the change process. They shape the means and the ends from planning through execution to institutionalization. Table 1 conveys a progression through which the goals and components of an innovation proceed during the change process (Herriott & Gross, 1979).

Components of an innovation

Some key components of an effective innovation are listed in the left column of Table 1. While these components have a research basis, other similar lists could be constructed. The key criterion for any such list is that the pieces create a coherent whole that addresses the major activities of teaching, learning, administering, and supervising and that has been demonstrated to yield improvements in those activities.

Validated instructional materials. Curriculum materials become validated when they are used by teachers and students and are found to produce the results claimed by the authors of the materials. Validated curriculum materials should play a central role in guiding student/teacher interactions. These interactions shape the learning that takes place. Thus, the quality of curriculum materials plays a crucial role in any attempt to increase student achievement. Since major change is almost always psychologically painful, the participants should end up as better teachers. This success not only is fair recompense for the pain resulting from change, but also is essential to maintain the innovation and create a school climate favorably dis-

Table 1
Products and processes of school improvement

	Exploration (Describe goal and list components of innovation)	Strategic planning (Refine goal and flesh out each component)	Implementation (Execute innovation)	Institutionalization ("Should you be so lucky")
Product (Goals)				
1. Who?				
2. Where?				
3. What?				
Components				
1. Validated curriculum				
2. Monitoring teacher performance				
3. Monitoring student performance				
4. Specific, concrete, constructive staff development				
5. Time				
6. Incentives				

posed toward subsequent change. Selecting validated materials increases the likelihood that both students and teachers will be rewarded. Using a validated curriculum also reduces the risk of an innovation failing. This is critical, since a failed innovation not only discredits the current innovation, but also contributes to cynicism about school improvement.

Monitoring teachers. Observing teachers can yield information that helps teachers solve problems. The information is not intended for formal evaluation. Behaviors that would be appropriate for monitoring range from the way a teacher arranges the physical environment of the classroom to the extent and nature of teacher responses to student errors. The physical arrangement can reveal whether the placement of lower performing students is adequate (that is, whether they are seated near the teacher where they can be heard and responded to). Another behavior might be how often and which students respond. Frequent responses allow teachers to make better decisions about how much content to present and which content merits additional explanation or practice. The skill levels of students who respond frequently reveal a teacher's expectations for different students. The ways in which teachers respond to student errors indicate the teacher's sophistication in diagnosing and remedying student errors.

Monitoring student performance. Student success rate on assignments, typically in the form of percent correct responses, is one of two major measures of student performance. The other is the content covered. One measure addresses quality of work done, the other quantity of work done. Both are important. Students must acquire a variety of knowledge and skills. This acquisition requires both proficiency (success level) and breadth (content covered).

If monitoring of student performance is to contribute to improvements in instruction, the monitoring must be done periodically during the year, while constructive action still can be taken. Schools traditionally collect mastery and content covered information at the end of the year, so the results often are not available until summer. If mastery and content coverage data are collected monthly, the results can be used in staff development activities. (See Gersten, Carnine, & White, 1984, for illustrations of student monitoring procedures.)

Informal assessment systems include classroom observations: noting whether extra time and attention are given to at risk students, looking at whether transition times are orderly or whether time is wasted, and reviewing workbooks to determine students' accuracy levels and their rate of progress.

Staff development. Being aware of the varying levels of teacher performance and student learning is futile unless the information can be used constructively. Teachers cannot be expected to make major changes without competent help from someone. The research on educational innovations has documented the importance of quality resource support and inservice training on a continuous, sustained basis (Fullan & Pomfret, 1977). The types of support suggested by the research include various features (Berman &

McLaughlin, 1978; Emrick, Peterson, & Agarwala-Rogers, 1977; Hall & Loucks, 1977; Herriott & Gross, 1979; Yin, Heald, & Vogel, 1977).

- Concrete, teacher specific activities (e.g., skill practice, teaching demonstrations, coaching).
- Ongoing training throughout implementation.
- Resource materials at the "how to" level.
- Regular interactions among peers.
- Regular interactions in the classroom with external resource consultants.

Conventional staff development and inservice training are viewed with contempt by both teachers and administrators, with good reason. The expectations for inservice outcomes are low, with content marginally useful. In a review of the inservice literature, Joyce and Showers (1980) hypothesize that an inservice session with a lecture on theory has minimal transfer into the classroom. The addition of demonstrations and role playing produce only modest increases in transfer. Joyce and Showers suggest that only with the addition of coaching, with direct links to what goes on in the classroom, will inservice be productive.

Coaching (personal, individualized staff development) is crucial to any innovation that requires major change on the part of teachers. The teacher effectiveness literature provides a framework for effective staff development. This staff development process is explained and illustrated in Table 2. The parallels between effective teaching and effective staff development should be apparent. Coaches, like teachers, diagnose, establish priorities, and remedy errors. Good remedies, whether devised by a teacher or a coach, include models, guided practice with extensive feedback, a shift from high to low structure, review (follow ups), large amounts of academic learning time, and encouragement for success.

Time. Much has been written about how little time is devoted to academics in school, and not all of that time is used well (Rosenshine, 1979). Lost time cannot be retrieved or revised. Indifference, poor planning, discipline problems, and extracurricular activities are major abusers of time. Establishing a schoolwide management system is often a useful starting point (see Paine et al., 1983, and Sprick, 1986, for suggestions on reducing wasted time).

Table 2
Individualized staff development

Step	Example
State problem. Articulate what needs to be changed.	"When the teacher asked the students to summarize a story, they gave random details."
Diagnose. An instructional problem almost always is complex. What are the causes?	(1) The stories are too difficult for the students. (2) The teacher isn't modeling a process students can use to learn to summarize other stories.
Set priorities. Not all causes can be addressed at once. What action will have the greatest immediate effect? What next?	Reading the current, more complex story is a reasonable goal, but not the first priority. The teacher should first teach a process for summarization with easier stories.
Remedy. Specify the instructional steps the teacher might use to reach the first priority.	Teach story grammar questions with a teacher model and guided practice (Carnine et al., 1985).
Explain. Discuss with the teacher the problem, diagnosis, priority, and remedy. The explanation must address the problem at hand and must serve as an example of the problem, diagnosis, priority, and remedy process for the teacher. The explanation must be clear, concise, and tactful.	"I'd like to focus on one of the most difficult instructional tasks in reading — summarization. The students are offering unorganized details from a story as a summary. They may be doing this because the story is somewhat complicated with subplots. I'd recommend presenting easier stories and modeling a series of questions students can ask themselves to generate a summary."
Model and practice. Since this is a substantial remedy, the model would occur after the reading period. If several teachers were having similar problems teaching summarization, a group inservice would be appropriate.	"First, let me explain the questions for teaching summarization and show how they can be used in a story....Now you figure out how the questions could be used in this story....For this story, I'll be a student. Ask me the questions just like you would ask a student....Basically a good job. You did leave out the questions about...."
Follow up. After the teacher has had several class periods to practice the remedy with students, a followup observation is needed, both to give additional feedback and to convey the importance of implementing the strategy.	"The students' summaries are much closer to the main ideas than they were the last time I observed. I particularly like your questions about....However, you still leave out a question about ....Next time, have the students summarize some of the more difficult stories you were having them read last week."

Carnine

Table 2
Individualized staff development (continued)

Step	Example
Encourage. Acknowledge well conceived and executed instruction, but do not give false praise.	"Since you've just about solved the summarization problem with easier stories, here's an idea for how to handle subplots....Try to find at least three stories with subplots so students have enough practice on that type of story."

Incentives. Most discussions acknowledge that few forms of incentives are available for well deserving teachers. Administrators, using discretionary funds and power, can channel money for conference travel and extra supplies or use assignments (e.g., cafeteria supervision) as reinforcement or punishment (Morris et al., 1981). Lacking in discussions of incentives (besides a paucity of useful ideas) is an explanation of why principals would dispense consequences according to how teachers improve students' achievements. One explanation (given earlier) is that administrators who violate the status quo to innovate in serious ways are acting heroically.

A key aspect of this heroism is building obligations. Edmonds, Hersh, Joyce, and others describe the outcome of such a system of obligations as a school climate conducive to continual improvement. The obligations range from public ceremonies and awards to exchange of goods (e.g., different groups from a staff prepare a meal for the entire staff).

Stages in the change process

The components of an innovation take shape through the change process. In the exploration stage (see Table 1), the goals of an innovation are first described and the components of the innovation are listed, though not the specifics of each component. The most prevalent barriers to arise during exploration are attempts to discredit the innovation. If the innovation is discredited, the change process halts. During the strategic planning stage, the details of the goals and of the innovation are settled. At this time, delays are commonly encountered. The implementation stage sets the innovation in place. Distortion during implementation is most likely to occur in using the curriculum and conducting staff development. Finally, for the institutionalization phase, discontinuation is the prime barrier.

In discussing goals during the exploration stage, leaders can rely on the traditional categories of who? where? and what? These discussions will largely determine the significance of the goal, for example, improving students' comprehension of short stories.

Who?   Low performing sixth graders

Where? In reading classes

What? Will give one story grammar based summary of a short story each week.

Goals become denigrated when school effectiveness methods are treated as ends themselves, as in behavior management plans that ignore academic goals.

Who?   Low performing sixth graders

Where? In language arts classes

What? Will not be disruptive.

Learning must be an ultimate goal of any attempt to establish and maintain order.

As part of the strategic planning stage, teachers and administrators need to be informed about the innovation, observe it, and make their decisions about implementation. Serious change takes two years to implement and two to four years after that to institutionalize. Rushing the introduction of an innovation is usually counterproductive because it can cause problems that remain throughout the entire four to six year process.

After a timeline is in place, leaders review the availability of resources. If time and money are lacking to support the innovation as broadly conceived, reduce its scope or abandon it altogether. Sometimes abandoning an innovation in the early stages is necessary. A staff development project built around intensive in class supervision is not viable unless a competent supervisor can work with teachers in their classrooms. If money isn't available for this supervisor, the innovation should be abandoned before both time and enthusiasm have been wasted.

Treating the components of an innovation as a system provides checks and balances. By devising simple, cost efficient measures of student success and content covered, vagaries in the curriculum might be identified. If the planning group cannot agree on what students should know or be able to do after completing six weeks of study, the curriculum planning needs to be more specific.

Another decision to make early in the strategic planning stage is who will carry out the innovation. Possibly only volunteer teachers from some grades or subjects will be involved initially. Careful selection of those volunteers is the easiest way to ensure a successful implementation. The first year should be used to demonstrate the potency of the innovation and to locate advocates for the innovation. The planning should take into account expanding the innovation to encompass an intact organizational group—at least a grade or subject within a school. Uninvolved peers are prime sources of pressure to discontinue an innovation. Starting out small enough to succeed may allow the innovation to grow large enough to survive.

The transportability of the innovation should be kept in mind throughout the strategic planning. If it is intended to be used by teachers with diverse interests and skills, the innovation should not be designed for just the initial volunteers, who may be more motivated and skilled than other teachers. Planners should remember that the demands of the curriculum and the support to be given through staff development should allow teachers to successfully implement the innovation.

The importance of teachers experiencing success when they implement an innovation cannot be overstressed. When substantial changes in student behavior are being sought, teacher success in making those changes may be a prerequisite for increased expectations. Gersten et al. (1986) found that teacher expectations for urban students' reading achievement rose only after the teachers implemented the innovation for seven months and saw larger than expected gains in reading performance. This finding implies that in addition to being coaxed and cajoled into implementing new procedures, teachers need to be coached to behave in new ways before they believe the new methods are worthwhile. An assertive stance during implementation entails certain necessary risks. The risks should be minimized as much as possible by an emphasis on using validated components in the innovation. The costs of change are high, so untried approaches and the failure they may bring are best avoided. The innovation succeeds only if students, teachers, and administrators succeed.

Setting a tone that conveys a seriousness of purpose and commitment to success is a crucial objective for the first stage of implementation. This introduction usually occurs during an inservice session. Administrators should advocate the innovation and should state the form of their support (e.g., performance in implementing the innovation is being incorporated in the district's goals for annual evaluations). A demonstration that staff development is going to help teachers solve problems means convincing the staff that the lecture format for staff development has been abandoned. Participants must see that staff development has changed and that new methods will help teachers solve problems in working with their students. The goal is to create a sense of community based on harder work, less autonomy, and a renewed belief in the role and value of schooling.

The day to day activities of the implementation are the most important part of the entire change process. (These activities were discussed in earlier sections on components of the innovation and managerial responsibilities of the change agent.) The details involved in a major change effort are enormous. Leaders who ensure that these details are implemented will not necessarily be seen as heroes. Innovators in the past were not necessarily treated kindly either. "Primitive tribes do not necessarily welcome radical ideas; they are quite capable of resisting an innovation even if it is demonstrably beneficial, and of putting to death the would be innovator as a sorcerer" (Hawkins, 1965, p. 35).

References

Anderson, R., St. Pierre, R., Proper, E., and Stebbins, L. Pardon us, but what was the question again. *Harvard Educational Review,* 1978, *48,* 161-170.

Argyris, C., and Schon, D. *Theory into practice: Increasing professional effectiveness.* San Francisco, CA: Jossey-Bass, 1974.

Berman, P., and McLaughlin, M.W. *Federal programs supporting educational change.* Volume 4, *The findings in review.* Santa Monica, CA: Rand Corporation, 1975.

Berman, P., and McLaughlin, M.W. *Federal programs supporting educational change.* Volume 8, *Implementation and sustaining motives.* Santa Monica, CA: Rand Corporation, 1978.

Burlingame, M. *Coordination, control, and facilitation of instruction within schools.* Paper presented at School Organization and Effects Conference of the National Institute of Education, San Diego, 1978.

Carlson, R.O. *Environmental constraints and organizational consequences: The public school and its clients.* Chicago: NSSE Yearbook, University of Chicago Press, 1964.

Carnine, D., and Kinder, D. Teaching low-performing students to apply generative and schema strategies to narrative and expository material. *Remedial and Special Education,* 1986, *6* (1), 20-30.

Carnine, D., and Silbert, J. *Direct instruction reading.* Columbus, OH: Charles Merrill, 1979.

Centra, J.A., and Porter, D.A. School and teacher effects: An interrelational model. *Review of Educational Research,* 1980, *50,* 274-291.

Chall, J. *Learning to read: The great debate.* New York: McGraw-Hill, 1967.

Charters, W.W., and Jones, J. On the risk of appraising nonevents in program evaluation. *Educational Researcher,* 1973, *2,* 5-7.

Clark, D.L., Lotto, L.S., and McCarthy, M.M. Factors associated with success in urban elementary schools. *Phi Delta Kappan,* 1980, *61,* 467-470.

Cohen, E.G. *Coordination, control, and facilitation of instruction in schools.* Working paper for the conference on school organization and its effect on student outcomes, San Diego, January 1978.

Cohen, E.G., Miller, R.H., Bredo, A., and Duckworth, K. *Principal role and teacher morale under varying organizational conditions.* Research Monograph. Stanford, CA: Stanford Center for Research and Development in Teaching, 1977.

Cohen, M.D., March, J.G., and Olsen, J.P. A garbage can model of organizational choice. *Administrative Science Quarterly,* 1972, *17,* 1-25.

Coleman, J.S., Campbell, E.Q., Hobson, C.J., McPartland, J., Mood, A.M., Weinfield, F.D., and York, R.C. *Equality of educational opportunity.* Washington, DC: U.S. Government Printing Office, 1966.

Corwin, R.G. *Reform and organizational survival: The teacher corps as an instrument of educational change.* New York: John Wiley & Sons, 1973.

Cronin, D.P. *Implementation study, year 2: Instructional staff interviews.* Los Altos, CA: John A. Emrick, 1980.

Datta, L.E. Changing times: The study of federal programs supporting educational change and the case for local problem solving. *Teachers College Record,* 1980, 101-115.

Denham, C., and Lieberman, A. (Eds.). *Time to learn.* Washington, DC: U.S. Department of Education, National Institute of Education, 1980.

Derr, B.C., and Deal, T.E. Toward a contingency theory of change in education: Organizational structure, processes, and symbolism. *Sage annual review of social and educational change.* Beverly Hills, CA: Sage, 1978.

Dornbush, S.D., and Scott, W.R. *Evaluation and the exercise of authority.* San Francisco, CA: Jossey-Bass, 1975.

Duke, D.L. Environmental influences on classroom management. In D.L. Duke (Ed.), *Classroom management,* Seventy-Eighth Yearbook of the National Society for the Study of Education. Chicago: University of Chicago Press, 1979.

Dunn, P. *Fact sheet, number one.* Eugene, OR: University of Oregon, ERIC Clearinghouse on Educational Management, 1980.

Edmonds, R. Effective schools for the urban poor. *Educational Leadership,* 1979, 15-24.

Emrick, J.A., Peterson, S.M., and Agarwala-Rogers, R. *Evaluation of the National Diffusion Network: Findings and recommendations.* Menlo Park, CA: Stanford Research Institute, 1977.

Forbes, R.H. Test score advances among Southeastern students: A possible bonus of government intervention? *Phi Delta Kappan,* 1981, *62,* 332-334.

Fullan, M., and Pomfret, A. Research on curriculum and instruction implementation. *Review of Educational Research,* 1977, *47,* 335-397.

Gaynor, A.L., Barrows, L., and Klenke, W. *A systems dynamics model of implementation of an innovation.* Madison, WI: Wisconsin Research and Development Center for Individualized Schooling, University of Wisconsin, 1980.

Georgious, P. The goal paradigm and notes toward a counterparadigm. *Administrative Science Quarterly,* 1973, *18,* 291-310.

Gersten, R., Carnine, D., and White, W.H.T. The pursuit of clarity: Direct instruction and applied behavior analysis. In W. Heward, T.E. Heron, D.S. Hill, and J. Trap-Porter (Eds.), *Focus on behavior analysis in education.* Columbus, OH: Charles Merrill, 1984.

Gersten, R., Carnine, D., Zoref, L., and Cronin, D. A multifaceted study of change in seven inner city schools. *Elementary School Journal,* 1986, *86* (3), 257-276.

Gilbert, T.F. *Human competence.* New York: McGraw-Hill, 1978.

Hall, G.E., and Loucks, S.F. A developmental model for determining whether the treatment is actually implemented. *American Educational Research Journal,* 1977, *14* (3), 263-276.

Hawkins, G.S. *Stonehenge decoded.* New York: Dell, 1965.

Herriott, R.E., and Gross, N. *The dynamics of planned educational change.* Berkeley, CA: McCutchan, 1979.

Hersh, R.H., Carnine, D., Gall, M., Stockard, J., Carmack, M.A., and Gannon, P. *The education professions and the enhancement of classroom productivity.* Eugene, OR: University of Oregon, CEPM Education Professions Committee, 1981.

Howell, B. Profile of the principalship. *Educational Leadership,* 1981, *38,* 333-336.

Jencks, C. *Who gets ahead? The determinants of economic success in America.* New York: Basic Books, 1979.

Jencks, C. et al. *Inequality: A reassessment of the effect of family and schooling in America.* New York: Basic Books, 1972.

Joyce, B., and Showers, B. Improving inservice training: The messages of research. *Educational Leadership,* 1980, 379-385.

Lortie, D. The balance of control and autonomy in elementary school teaching. In A. Etzioni (Ed.), *The semiprofessions and their organization: Teachers, nurses, social workers.* New York: Free Press, 1969.

Lyons, G. Why teachers can't teach. *Phi Delta Kappan,* 1980, *2,* 108-112.

March, J.G. American public school administration: A short analysis. *School Review,* 1978, *86,* 217-250.

Mazzeralla, J.A. *The principal's role as an instructional leader.* Burlingame, CA: Association of California School Administrators, 1977.

Meyer, J.W., Scott, W.R., and Deal, T.E. *Institutional and technical sources of organizational structure explaining the structure of educational organizations.* Paper prepared for a conference on Human Service Organizations, Center for Advanced Study in the Behavior Sciences, Stanford, California, 1979.

Morris, V.C., Crowson, R., Hurwitz, E., and Porter-Gehrie, C. *The urban principal: Discretionary decision making in a large educational organization.* Chicago: University of Illinois, 1981.

Ogbu, J.U. *An ecological approach to the study of school effectiveness.* Paper presented at the National Institute of Education's Conference on School Organization and Effects in San Diego, 1978.

Ozenne, D. et al. United States Office of Education. *Annual evaluation report on programs administered by the U.S. Office of Education, FY 1975.* Washington, DC: Capital Publications, Educational Resources Division, 1976.

Paine, S., Radicchi, J., Rosellini, L., Deutchman, L., and Darch, C. *Structuring your classrooms for academic success.* Champaign, IL: Research Press, 1983.

Parrish, R. *Discontinuation of innovation programs through the NDN.* Unpublished doctoral dissertation, University of Oregon at Eugene, 1981.

Phillips, D.C. What do the researcher and the practitioner have to offer each other? *Educational Researcher,* 1980, *9,* 17-20.

Pincus, J. Incentives for innovation in the public schools. *Review of Educational Research,* 1974, 113-144.

Rosenshine, B. Content, time, and direct instruction. In P.L. Peterson and H.J. Walberg (Eds.), *Research on teaching: Concepts, findings, and implications.* Berkeley: McCutchan, 1979.

Rowan, B. Bureaucratization in the institutional environment: The case of California Public Schools, 1930-1970. In M.R. Davis, T.E. Deal, J.W. Merey, B. Rowan, W.R. Scott, and E.A. Stackhouse (Eds.), *The structure of educational systems: Explorations in the theory of loosely coupled organizations.* Stanford, CA: Stanford Center for Research and Development in Teaching, 1977.

Ryan, W. *Blaming the victim.* New York: Vintage, 1971.

Salley, C., McPherson, R.B., and Baehr, M.E. What principals do: A preliminary occupational analysis. *Consortium Currents,* 1975, *2,* 1-10.

Sarason, S. *The culture of the school and the problem.* Boston: Allyn and Bacon, 1971.

Snow, R.W. Representative and quasirepresentative designs for research on teaching. *Review of Educational Research,* 1974, *44,* 265-290.

Sprick, R. *Secondary school management.* Englewood Cliffs, NJ: Prentice-Hall, 1986.

Stallings, J. Implementation and child effects of teaching practices in Follow Through classrooms. *Monographs of the Society for Research in Child Development,* 1975, *40,* 7-8.

Stevens, R., and Rosenshine, B. Advance in research on teaching. *Exceptional Education Quarterly,* 1981, *2,* 1-9.

Tikunoff, W., Berliner, D., and Rist, R. *An ethnographic study of the forty classrooms of the beginning teacher evaluation study known sample.* Technical Report No. 75-10-5. San Francisco, CA: Far West Laboratory for Educational Research and Development, 1975.

Tomlinson, T.M. The troubled years: An interpretive analysis of public schooling since 1950. *Phi Delta Kappan,* 1981, *62,* 373-376.

Tucker, H.J., and Zeigler, L.H. *Professionals versus the public: Attitudes, communication, and response in school districts.* New York: Longman, 1980.

Weick, K.E. Educational organizations as loosely coupled systems. *Administrative Science Quarterly,* 1976, *21,* 1-19.

White, E. Education's troubled crusade: No easy victories, no lasting defeats. Review of D. Ravitch's *The troubled crusade. Education Week,* January 1984, 8-17.

Wolcott, H.F. *Teachers vs. technocrats: An educational innovation in anthropological perspective.* Eugene, OR: Center for Educational Policy and Management, University of Oregon, 1977.

Wolf, W. The state of urban schools: New data on an old problem. *Urban Education,* 1978, *13* (2), 179-194.

Wyant, S.H. *Of principals and projects.* Reston, VA: Association of Teacher Educators, 1980.

Yin, R.K., Heald, K.A., and Vogel, M.E. *Tinkering with the system.* Lexington, MA: Lexington Books, 1977.

Part two

Case studies in change: Making it happen

Prelude

I n this chapter, Ramona Hao speaks with the authority of practical wisdom; she has served for
several years as both a consultant and a trainer of
consultants in the Kamehameha Early Education
Project (KEEP) in Honolulu. She describes the problems she and her colleagues have encountered and
the processes they have used to export the program
developed at the home KEEP site in Honolulu to public
school settings throughout Hawaii. There are two
kinds of information to glean from her presentation:
There is much to be learned from the specific approaches used in KEEP to help teachers adapt to new
techniques, and her presentation illustrates broad
principles of institutional change. For example, the
issue of feedback loops in knowledge dissemination,
introduced as a research concept in Chapter 2, is
discussed as a very real problem in transporting the
KEEP model to other sites. And the issue of how direct
to be in bringing about change (echoing the dilemma
of directed development or mutual adaptation introduced in Chapters 2 and 3) appears throughout Hao's
presentation.

Research and development model for improving reading instruction

W hen we first founded the Kamehameha Early Education Program (KEEP) to find a way to help Hawaiian children do better in school, we envisioned a curriculum, a set of materials, and a set of teaching behaviors. Initially, we failed to address two questions. First, could we get schools and teachers to agree to use the program? Second, could we teach them to do so effectively and efficiently? We assumed that if we could develop a program that produced the desired results with children, the rest would be easy – schools and teachers would be knocking down our doors demanding the program. Unfortunately, it has not worked that way. Bringing about change in one classroom or even in one person is seldom easy; bringing it about in large numbers of teachers and even larger numbers of students has taken as much research, time, and effort as was needed for the development of the original program.

This chapter will focus on the change we are trying to bring about through the dissemination of a reading program developed by a research and development institution. I will describe the institution and the mechanism set up for program dissemination, the method by which we introduce change to schools, five major problems we encountered and the ways we are attempting to solve them, and an effective model for change when working with teachers to help them adapt to a new program.

It is necessary to understand the nature of the particular research and dissemination institution, its goals, and the complex nature of the program itself in order to understand the problems that have developed as the dissemination of the program to schools has grown. Although the program is currently being used by about eighty teachers throughout Hawaii, the planned dissemination rate has been delayed by the problems described in the third section.

The change model in section four has evolved out of experience, intuition, research, and trial and error. Its use has produced change, and, when paired with the accompanying interaction techniques and consulting rules, has produced a number of productive, mutually satisfying relationships with teachers.

Setting

About 100 years ago, the last Princess of Hawaii left her extensive estate for the education of Hawaiian children. The Kamehameha Schools serve as a low cost private school for educating high achieving Hawaiian and part Hawaiian children in the state.

In recent years, the trustees of the estate have become increasingly concerned about the estimated 58,000 Hawaiian and part Hawaiian children in the state's middleclass oriented public schools. Many of these students are low achievers, with all the behavior problems that accompany low achievement. An extension division was created to do more for these non Kamehameha students. It offered alienated teenagers cultural programs, tutorial programs, and summer school.

The trustees felt that these programs were only stopgap measures and that a long term commitment was needed to prevent these problems. Therefore, fourteen years ago, KEEP began as an attempt to find out why these five to eleven year old Hawaiian children were doing so poorly in their public school setting and how and what to teach to enable them to succeed in school. KEEP brought together teachers, anthropologists, psychologists, linguists, and curriculum specialists to study Hawaiian children and their relationships at home and at school. After six years of research (Tharp et al., 1984), KEEP's efforts culminated in a reading and language arts curriculum, a group of teaching strategies, and a culturally compatible set of techniques for interacting with the students; that is, techniques that capitalized on (rather than conflicted with) the natural learning and interaction styles of Hawaiian students (Jordan, 1981). The combination of all these elements produced results visible in direct observation of classrooms and students and in criterion referenced and standardized testing. The results were so stable that we could virtually guarantee them if a teacher implemented the program as it was designed (Tharp, 1982). As the KEEP Reading Program began to be disseminated successfully in a few classrooms in the public schools, interest in extending a similar process for research downward to preschool and, ultimately, to infant care, grew, and KEEP (the program for five to eleven year olds) became just a part of the Kamehameha Schools Center for Development of Early Education. It remains the largest part of the Center, since the programs for the zero to two and three to four year old children are still in the infancy stage. As can be seen from this brief description of our organization, our goals extend far beyond the research and development of a program. However, that ongoing research effort remains at the heart of our work as we try to make a positive change in the academic progress of some 20,000 Hawaiian and part Hawaiian elementary students on the five major islands of Hawaii. It is, however, the change attempted through the dissemination of the program to public school sites that is the focus of this discussion. Change within the institution will be referred to only as it affects this external dissemination.

Training and dissemination

The Training and Dissemination Unit of KEEP performs five functions: training new consultants, supervising consultants in the KEEP lab school, supervising field sites, conducting training research, and planning visitations to home or field sites.

Currently, five field sites are located at five schools on three islands. Each field site has a permanent staff, the size of which is based on the number of teachers at each school.

The remainder of this chapter focuses on the changes we are trying to bring about at each of the field sites. The KEEP office is usually located in a school classroom. A manager at each site reports to the Director of Training and Dissemination and is responsible for KEEP operations there. Roughly one consultant and one trainer assistant serve each five teachers who use the program.

The consultant and the trainer assistant train and support teachers using the KEEP Reading Program. Because we believe teachers are the key to student learning, our training efforts are concentrated on the teacher. Teachers use their training to effect change in students.

The consultant runs workshops, observes each teacher for at least an hour a week, gives feedback on these observations, and meets with the teacher for at least one half hour weekly. The consultant also develops curriculum materials, meets with other consultants, receives further training, carries out research in planned variations of the program, and sometimes substitutes for a teacher who is out of the classroom for training.

The trainer assistant (TA) is an aide who supports the efforts of the consultant. The TA administers the criterion referenced testing program, an essential and time consuming part of the KEEP Reading Program. The TA also observes teacher and student behaviors, types language experience stories, copies materials for teachers and consultants, and prepares workshop materials.

Program

The KEEP Reading Program is based on a set of reading objectives that guide the teacher. There are six critical elements (Tharp, 1982) to the program, which has been developed around this set of objectives.

1. An emphasis on comprehension instruction at all levels.
2. Daily small group reading instruction with ten to twelve learning centers where students work independently while the teacher leads the small groups.
3. Emphasis on the teacher as a motivator for learning. This includes a positive approach to classroom management and responsiveness to student speech and ideas.
4. Continuous monitoring and feedback of student achievement.
5. Diagnostic/prescriptive instruction.

6. A quality control system for monitoring teacher instruction.

Note that the program is not just a set of objectives or of teaching methods; it is a combination of these along with a classroom organization and management system and a style of responsive interaction between the teacher and students. It is not a program that can be learned by attending several workshops. Because much of the program involves learning how to be a thoughtful, flexible, problem solving teacher, it requires a great deal of practice, questioning, learning, and redirection toward a new set of interaction styles in order to master the program.

System for introducing change

When trustees and administrators decide there are resources to open a new dissemination site at a public school, three factors are considered: Is the population of the school at least 25 percent part Hawaiian? Is the program needed? (State standardized testing results provide this information.) Are any trained consultants available to move into the area permanently (or temporarily) until personnel from that area can be hired and trained? Each site has opened with one consultant and fewer than five teachers for the first year. The plan has been to start small and add more teachers and consultants in the second year.

When a potential site has been identified, a presentation describing the program is given to the district superintendent. Since Hawaii has a statewide school system, we have a blanket go ahead for this procedure from the State Superintendent and the State Board of Education, to whom we present yearly reports of progress and results. However, Department of Education (DOE) policy is to let each district, each school, and each teacher decide whether to use the program.

After we present the program to the district superintendent, we present it to the principal of the school. If the principal permits, we give a presentation for interested teachers who are under no obligation to sign up for the program.

In the presentation for the teachers, we emphasize change. Until now, the introduction of the program has required a change in philosophy, curriculum, instructional materials, and classroom management and organization systems. In the presentation, we discuss these program changes in relation to the change that will be seen in students, not only in test scores, but in their behavior and attitude toward the teacher, the school, and one another. We show videotapes of classrooms and children using the program and present test results from other sites. We close our presentation with a statement about what KEEP can and will do for the principal and teachers and what they need to do for KEEP, should they decide to join the program.

For a school to become a site, the principal must agree to support the teachers in the program and agree that the KEEP Reading and Language Arts Program will be the program for those teachers. The principal must also agree to release teachers from the classroom for three or four days a year for training (KEEP pays for substitutes and any other expenses, but needs permission to do so).

Teachers must accept KEEP's philosophy that reading is understanding and must agree to support the program. They also must agree to be observed frequently by KEEP site personnel, KEEP researchers, and personnel from other sites; to install each program element; and to support the program itself.

After the school presentation, we meet individually with interested teachers to answer any questions they may have. In addition, without obligation, we arrange for interested teachers to visit a KEEP site so they can see the program in action and talk with teachers already using the program.

Contract forms are left at the school and, while they are not binding, they do spell out the terms of the agreement. Teachers are told that they may drop out of the program at any time. (In five years, only two have done so.)

Problems and ways of dealing with them

In an organization that in ten years has grown from a staff of 14 to a staff of 200, problems have been numerous and varied. I will focus on the problems consultants encounter when they try to bring about change in teacher behavior.

KEEP has virtually every material resource known to the profession because money has not been a problem. KEEP also has had access to the best thinking in the profession. Not only is the staff highly qualified, but top consultants from several disciplines have evaluated KEEP's work and have provided input into the research design of the instructional program. Yet, there are still human and practical problems.

Guest/host relationship

The guest/host relationship between KEEP and the State Department of Education has produced its share of problems. As nonbinding agreements are negotiated by individual school districts, individual schools, and teachers, the process of finding new schools and teachers is extremely lengthy and sensitive. It takes at least a year of meetings, presentations, and teacher visitations to get permission to install the program in a new school.

All the teachers at field sites are volunteers. Volunteers are likely to be enthusiastic, willing to put in the time and effort necessary to learn and implement a new program, and to agree with KEEP's goals for the children and general philosophy of reading. On the other hand, volunteers may drop out of the program at any time with little or no motive. In addition, as the program expands at a school, some teachers may never volunteer. This may cause a split in the faculty that can be exacerbated by parental pressure. (There have been instances in which parents have wanted their children switched from non KEEP classrooms.)

There are other problems inherent in a guest/host working relationship. Regardless of previous agreements, these same teachers may now have two sets of goals they must meet, coming from both the old and the new programs. Often, instead of changing to a new reading program with its concomitant philosophy, goals, objectives, and methods, the teachers have to add these onto existing goals and objectives they already have to meet.

Consider the first grade teacher who has to meet all the objectives of the KEEP Reading Program, make sure the students pass at least four SRA levels, and read thirty books from an instructional library from the prior reading program. The teacher also may have to fill out record forms specifying which objectives in the new program transfer to the objectives in the old program.

Another disadvantage is the lack of control over the placement of teachers. In the guest/host relationship, a trained first grade teacher may be moved to a non KEEP sixth grade classroom and be unable to continue in the program (KEEP has not yet developed a reading program above the fourth grade).

In the past, we at KEEP have dealt with the problems occurring because of the guest/host relationship by simply accepting the problems and working around them. We are trying two new ways to deal with these problems. First, the principals of the laboratory schools are setting up a series of meetings with the DOE field site principals. These meetings will provide a forum for discussion, problem solving, and training about KEEP, its goals and philosophy, and the importance of ongoing research. Second, we have planned small conferences or retreats to bring together a district superintendent, the deputy superintendent, district field site principals, KEEP administrative personnel, and consultants from the district field sites to discuss both general and specific problems and to develop guidelines to enhance the working relationship.

Consultant-teacher stress

Much teacher stress comes from the basic changes being made in how the teacher relates to a consultant, how the teacher relates to other teachers and school staff, how students relate to other students, and how the teacher relates to the student.

Actually, in implementing the KEEP Reading Program, the basic culture of the school changes. There's a kind of culture shock produced as the basic interaction patterns change. The relationship between the teacher and the consultant is new; the teacher has had no access to this kind of help before. It becomes a very intense relationship as the consultant moves in and out of the teacher's classroom at will, often several times a day for brief periods. The teacher and the consultant meet regularly once a week, in addition to daily brief interactions about students, materials, and activities. Interaction among teachers using the same program increases as teamwork on planning, problem solving, and material development is encouraged. Communication with teachers who are not in the program decreases as pressures from the new program diminish opportunities for such communication. Teachers often begin to discuss not only problems about reading and language arts, but problems related to behavior management and parent complaints with the consultant, rather than with the administrator.

As the classroom organization and behavior management aspect of the KEEP Reading Program encourages students to talk to and to help others working at the same station (a culturally compatible part of the program), there is a change in the relationship among students. During the discussion in the small group direct instruction session, students are encouraged to listen and to react not only to the teacher but to one another. Both of these activities change the student/student and teacher/student interaction patterns. These changes produce stress for a teacher who has been used to a lecture/worksheet format, or a round robin oral reading teaching session with the remainder of the students doing individual work under a strict rule of no student talk whatsoever.

The high accountability inherent in the program itself is a major cause of teacher stress. Teachers are observed by consultants at least once a week. Results of the direct observations are given in meetings and used to make further decisions for the classroom and for teacher training. The data from quality control coding of teacher instructional behavior is graphed and discussed with the teacher weekly (Au & Hao, 1983). As soon as teachers think students have learned a particular skill, they are tested using criterion referenced tests. Teachers and students receive immediate feedback on the results of this testing. In addition, teachers receive quarterly reports of observation and criterion referenced data showing change data and comparisons with norm data. Midyear and at the end of each year, standardized reading tests are given and results shown to the teacher. This high accountability for teachers is unusual and often produces stress.

In addition to accountability, the complexity of the program may create stress. The program causes extra work for the teacher—learning new habits in responsive questioning of students, planning lessons, and developing language and thinking skills. Even highly motivated teachers find the extra work difficult and stressful; fortunately, they also find it worthwhile because they see positive changes in their students.

The biggest cause of stress for consultants is relieving the program stress teachers experience. Consultants are accountable to KEEP for results and must get these results without applying overt pressure that could be debilitating for a teacher.

Another cause of stress is the research based program itself. The program is always changing as new research and new data provide different content, emphasis, methods, and training techniques. Consultants must be flexible, but even those who react well in this constant state of change periodically show signs of stress or burnout.

There is no doubt that these major changes have a personal cost, both emotionally and intellectually. Some ways have been tried to alleviate this cost.

Substitutes are hired for three or four days a year so teachers can attend training sessions. At least one of these days is spent at the laboratory school. For sites on other islands, the teachers fly in for a one or two day training and observation session. This accomplishes two purposes—some relaxation from a demanding program and some feeling of attachment to the parent institution. We hold award banquets for each island in late spring each year and give certificates of achievement to the teachers. We write letters of appreciation and place them in the teachers' personnel files.

Job rotation has been effective in alleviating stress for consultants. We try to arrange for those who work at the sites to return to work at home base. This is not always possible, however, because of family and other personal commitments.

Consultants receive funds to travel to national conferences. In addition to temporarily relieving stress, conferences keep consultants up to date with new research, new teaching practices, and new materials.

Compensatory time also is arranged. Because extra time is needed at certain periods of the year to prepare for or even to run workshops and to write materials and reports, compensatory time is arranged for consultants to get away from the job periodically.

Hao

The problem of teacher/consultant stress in such a demanding, accountable program has not been solved. In fact, the organization has not always been as sensitive to this problem as it should have been. Ignoring the signs of stress has caused home and work related problems for teachers and consultants. The tendency has been to delegate more work to those who handle stress best; those who have stress problems often receive less work or a different (and perhaps more desired) position.

Materials and equipment

Equipment and supplies are necessary for teaching, supporting, and maintaining the KEEP Reading Program. There is a lack of instructional materials in many of the schools. Schools often need to acquire more basal readers and more tradebooks of varied reading levels in order to teach small reading groups of children at their instructional level. Because the Language Experience Approach is an integral part of the reading program, chart paper and thousands of index cards are needed. An office/testing area is necessary for the permanent KEEP staff hired for the school. Desks, chairs, file cabinets, typewriters, and duplicating equipment are necessary.

In spite of this, the problem of materials and equipment has been the easiest to solve. Basically, KEEP pays for everything needed for the program that the school ordinarily does not provide. Usually the school provides one basal series, duplicating materials, and other office materials. KEEP provides alternate basals at several reading levels for each classroom, extensive collections of tradebooks and expository reading materials, equipment for the office (except in rare circumstances), and duplicating equipment when access to the school equipment has proved difficult.

External validity of the program

Because the KEEP Reading Program was developed in a laboratory school, there was a question as to its external validity. The field testing of the program in two schools in 1978-1979 brought good results (Tharp, 1982), and the program dissemination began. However, the problem of external validity remains. The program is currently being used by more than eighty teachers in seven schools on three islands. As research continues at the laboratory school, several questions are being asked: Are all these teachers teaching what is considered to be the program? Is the program correctly installed in all classrooms? What effect do specific conditions and restraints have on the program at each of the different schools, with different populations, different teacher personalities, and different school characteristics? These are not easy questions to answer. The first indication of problems came in the third year of dissemination. As the number of consultants grew, variability of certain teachers' criterion referenced and standardized test scores also increased.

There had always been a feedback loop in the dissemination system. New ideas came from the researchers, the laboratory school, and the sites. As the program was implemented in the field, new ideas, practical adaptations, and feasibility evaluations were fed from the field back into the curriculum, research, and training components of the program. However, this feedback loop too often was dependent upon the interest, enthusiasm, and skill of the field consultant. At this point, it became necessary to institute several safeguards: essential features coding, field research, and training.

Essential features coding. A list was developed of what was thought to be the essential features of the KEEP Reading Program (Au & Blake, 1984). Each consultant observes each teacher six times a year, determining the presence or absence of the features in the classroom. The coding provides a guide for the consultant to use during observation and gives a good measure of whether all features of the program have been implemented.

Field research. It has been much easier for researchers to conduct research at the laboratory school than at field sites because there are resources for research (research assistance, video equipment, observation deck); teachers are hired with the expectation that they will facilitate research; and travel time and expense do not need to be considered. We have recognized the need for more field research and more will be done in the future.

Training. Certain recognized KEEP experts on specific topics often run workshops at all sites in order to be sure the information and the training are consistent. For instance, a language development researcher (or teacher who has been working closely with the researcher) may visit all sites during October to train teachers and consultants on a new method of eliciting verbal responses from students. This helps assure that the training at sites is consistent with that at home base and that research is actually incorporated into the current program.

Training of consultants

For the KEEP Reading Program to reach 11,500 Hawaiian students in thirty-five schools in fourteen years, the training of consultants becomes a key issue. Consultants are the key to dissemination of the program. They are expected to install the program and to deal with curriculum problems, the reading process, personal relations, group and individual student behavior, visitations, workshops, and talks to prospective teachers. In short, consultants need to be all things to all people.

The first consultants for the reading program were characterized by a broad background in teaching and a wide familiarity with the KEEP Reading Program; they not only taught the program but participated in its development. They were chosen as consultants because of their willingness, enthusiasm, and ability to work with other people. These first consultants had very little formal guidance; they were guided by past experience and intuition. We held regular meetings to discuss what worked and what did not. The principles developed by these first consultants, teachers, and researchers then became a part of the training of the next group of consultants, who began their work as apprentices to the experienced consultants.

As KEEP expanded to more classrooms in the public schools and we needed more consultants in the field, four things became apparent: We were unable to hire many experienced teachers; training consultants was a slow process that required at least two years of classroom teaching at the laboratory school prior to consultant apprenticeship; the apprentice model of training did not assure a good, new consultant; and not all good teachers make effective consultants.

Two characteristics of the school systems in Hawaii adversely affected our ability to hire experienced teachers. First, public school teachers are awarded tenure after teaching two years and one day. Second, for the past twelve years, few positions for teachers have opened up in the public schools. The teachers in Hawaii have tenured positions, making it financially disadvantageous for them to change employers. On the other hand, unemployed people with teaching degrees generally have little or no experience.

For new consultant trainees to become good teachers of the KEEP Reading Program, they had to teach a minimum of two years. This then presupposed plenty of classrooms for them to train in and consultants to train them to teach the program. A question arose: Was it necessary for consultant trainees to become highly skilled teachers in order to train and consult with teachers, or was only a good knowledge of the workings of the program necessary?

In the field, the apprentice model for consultant training had variable results. Some of the trainees proved effective, both in teacher/consultant relationships and in student outcome measures; other trainees developed problems in one or both areas. Varied results seemed to be related to two factors: the consultant to whom the trainee was apprenticed, and the personality and background of the trainee.

As several outstanding teachers in KEEP became consultants, we readily reached another conclusion—not all good teachers make good consultants. Different skills are involved in the two positions.

To develop a more efficient model for training, we interviewed teachers, consultants, aides, and administrators in a performance expectations study to develop a profile of characteristics of a good consultant (Shapiro & Sloat, 1984). Nineteen characteristics were identified. We knew that some of these characteristics, such as giving feedback, making reasonable demands on a teacher, content knowledge, and time management, could be taught to consultants. However, we also knew that some, such as learning ability, flexibility, stress tolerance, responsibility, and interpersonal skills (friendliness, sensitivity, and tact), were impossible, difficult, or expensive to teach to prospective consultants.

Using the knowledge from prior years' experience and from the Shapiro and Sloat study, we developed a highly selective hiring process and created a consultant training department. We try to hire consultant trainees who already possess many skills from the Shapiro and Sloat study.

The year long training program (Bogert, Sloat, & Kent, in press) of seminars and practicums concentrates on the training of the consultant. At the end of seven months in the training program, the trainees are assigned to field sites for two months of on site training.

There remains some variability in the expertise of consultants stemming from these new hiring and training processes, but they clearly have more knowledge of content, research, and the art of consulting than any consultants in the past. They have developed better working relationships with the home based researchers and teachers and a greater affinity for KEEP than consultants completely trained in the field. Most of the remaining problems in this area deal with adapting to different administrative policies and personal relationships at the sites.

Model for change

We believe that teachers learn in very much the same way students learn, an idea important to remember when we consult with teachers. The consultants should interact with teachers in the same way they want teachers to interact with students. This pattern serves three purposes: Consultants serve as models for teachers, teachers see that consultants "practice what they preach," and teachers experience the pupil's perspective of the interaction.

Interaction techniques basically are divided into four interrelated categories: grouping for instruction; responsive listening and teaching; using prior knowledge as the bridge to new knowledge; and building a high risk, high trust atmosphere in which to work.

Although many consultants prefer to work with teachers on a one to one basis, we find that a small group of three to five teachers meeting with the consultant to discuss problems, goals, and plans usually works better. In a one to one situation, the consultant may be overpowering; it is difficult for teachers to speak up and add new ideas when they consider the consultant an expert. However, in a small group, teachers soon learn to speak out and listen to one another's ideas as well as to the consultant's. These problem solving, teaching groups need to be large enough for good discussions, but small enough that shy teachers will not be overpowered by highly verbal fellow teachers.

These small groups work well for almost any problem solving, instructional, brainstorming meetings. It is necessary to meet individually only if the problem to be discussed is a sensitive issue involving one teacher or when direct observation data involving immediate change in a classroom are to be presented. When a teacher introduces a problem that is not occurring in other teachers' classrooms at that moment, the other teachers listen because they know that it probably will occur. In addition, going through the steps of problem identification, problem analysis, generation of alternative solutions, and deciding on a plan of action helps all the teachers practice using a problem solving model they can use to solve other problems in their own classrooms.

As with students, a list of preset questions and preset procedural steps seldom works. While it is absolutely necessary for a consultant to have goals, objectives, and a game plan from which to work, the consultant must be a good listener and must be responsive to both the teacher's felt needs and actual needs. For example, two teachers entering the program at the same time do not necessarily progress through the objectives at the same rate. One teacher may have problems remembering to validate students' predictions when doing Directed Listening Thinking Activities (DLTA) while the other teacher does it flawlessly from the beginning. The first teacher will need feedback and further instruction while the second one will need feedback only before going on to another objective.

In addition to varying the pacing of objectives and the amount of instruction, a consultant needs to respond to a teacher's immediate needs. A classroom management problem occurring right now is often more important to a teacher than how to execute, a language experience lesson. A good consultant deals with the problem either by discussing it and agreeing on its relative importance in the long term goals or by working on solving the problem and getting back to the matter at hand. Several factors need to be considered when deciding what to do: (1) the importance of the problem to the teacher,

(2) how that problem fits into the long range goals, (3) whether solving that problem depends on other skills the teacher does not yet have, and (4) whether the next objective depends on this problem being solved first. Of course, the teacher has to understand upon what data these decisions rest and should be included in the decision making process.

The instruction for students in the KEEP Reading Program is based on the principle "Comprehension is building bridges between the new and the known" (Pearson & Johnson, 1978, p. 24). The training of teachers is based on this same principle. Every experienced teacher knows a great deal about teaching. The consultant builds on what the teacher already knows. For instance, we teach classroom management skills for those teachers whose management skills are unsuccessful in keeping students on task and able to work cooperatively with other students in the classroom. If a teacher already has a successful classroom management style, training in this area is not necessary.

Teachers need a high risk, high trust atmosphere in which to work. It is important that teachers be able to express ideas and reactions freely. If a consultant is unaware of these or cannot take feedback from the teacher, problems will be shoved under the rug and will not surface until the problem has grown out of proportion. It is much easier to deal with problems while they are still small. From the very beginning, a consultant must be there to help the teacher, not to scold when things go wrong.

Model for change

Using the previously discussed interaction techniques, the consultant works with the teachers using the model for change. This model shows a series of tasks to be undertaken during the first year of the implementation of the program in a classroom.

Long term goal setting is the first step. Both the teacher and the consultant must agree on these long term goals. Because of the teacher's inexperience with the program, there is more consultant input than teacher input into this task; however, the teacher knows what the students need and has a general knowledge of the program.

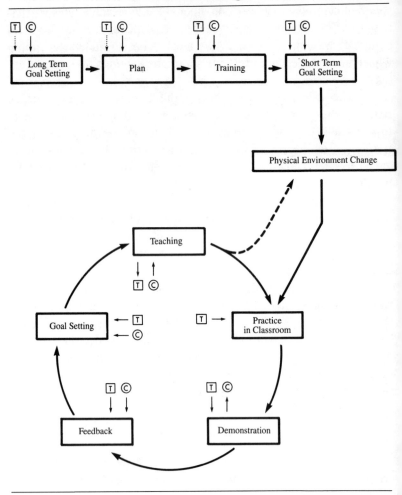

From the long term goals, a plan is developed for the year, again with a stronger input from the consultant because of the consultant's knowledge of the program. The teacher adds input on knowledge of school objectives, goals, time constraints, and the students. Again, there must be agreement on this plan.

At this point, training begins. Usually, initial training starts in a series of workshops given the week before school begins in the fall. All these workshops could be given by the teachers' consultant. However, other consultants and researchers from KEEP often participate in the workshops. This gives teachers the opportunity to meet and interact with more KEEP personnel, thus decreasing the feeling of isolation from the KEEP institution. In addition, bringing in experts lends more importance to the training. However, the site consultants do part of the training in order to give themselves credibility with the teachers. Although this training should be interactive with the teacher an active participant, the consultant is imparting knowledge and skills to the teacher.

After this series of workshops, the teacher and consultant set short term goals. At this point, the input is much more equally divided between the consultant and the teacher(s). They work together to decide what their goals are for the first day, the first week, and for the necessary skills to be used in the classroom. They discuss lesson plans, classroom set up, rules, and expectations for the children.

Because the combination of teaching and management behaviors in KEEP are often different from what has been used in other programs, the teacher needs cues to react differently. A physical environment change can operate as that cue for both teachers and students. For example, in the first two to four weeks of school, the teacher introduces the program in a series of phases. For each of these phases, content and management goals are set and lesson plans developed.

In one phase, teaching is carried out in large group sessions interspersed with independent work sessions. The classroom environment is set up to cue the teacher to large group instruction and to "floating" around the room observing and helping students establish on task and interpersonal behaviors. Materials, desks, tables, books, boxes, and wastebaskets are placed strategically to help remind the teacher to look for and reinforce certain behaviors in the students.

In another phase, classroom organization is changed in order to cue teacher and students to new or more advanced behaviors necessary for a two center classroom.

When the environment has been changed to accommodate the full program organization of ten to twelve learning centers (with one serving as the instructional center), the environment remains stable the rest of the year.

The remainder of the change model is repeated throughout the year.

1. The teacher practices a behavior, a new method, or whatever agreed upon activity or goal has been set.
2. The teacher demonstrates the behavior in the classroom for the consultant.
3. The teacher and the consultant meet as soon as possible after the demonstration. During this feedback session, the teacher discusses feelings about the behavior, how the students reacted, how the behavior could be improved, and how to proceed. The consultant elicits this information from the teacher and adds to the teacher's feedback with observation data taken during the demonstration.
4. After the feedback portion of the meeting, the teacher and consultant make further plans and set more short term goals based on feedback previously discussed.
5. Depending on the procedure and goals just set, teaching by the consultant occurs. This teaching may take several forms.

Modeling. Modeling of a procedure, a method, or a behavior may be done by live modeling in the teacher's classroom, role playing, using a videotape model, or by observing fellow teachers in their classrooms. If at all possible when using live classroom demonstration, a consultant should sit with and guide the teacher through the observation of this procedure in order to focus on the relevant behaviors.

Instruction. Instruction is telling the teacher what or how to do something. The consultant most often instructs directly but may have the teacher read material in order to carry out a procedure. For small details, simply telling a teacher what to do is effective and efficient.

Questioning. Using a line of well structured questions, the consultant may elicit from and, therefore, "teach" the teacher a new skill or method.

Cognitive restructuring. In cognitive restructuring (Tharp & Gallimore, 1983), the consultant provides explanations that organize and justify what is being learned. This is an important aspect of the teaching process, since teachers need to know how and when to apply the skills learned and why. This will help the teacher when applying the skills in new situations.

Relationship model

When a definite program is being installed (as with KEEP), it works well to begin with a consultant dominated relationship. However, once the program is installed, the relationship must change to that of a collegial partnership. In order to make this change, the teacher must gain program knowledge; know how (the skill of how and when to apply that knowledge); and problem solving skills. Therefore, the task of fostering these skills while installing specific elements of the program rests with the consultant. The consultant imparts knowledge and expertise in such a way that the teacher gains not only the knowledge or content itself but also knowledge of why, how, and when to use it. The consultant accomplishes this by using a judicious mixture of the four training forms: modeling, instructing, questioning, and cognitive restructuring.

The real goal of this relationship model is to increase the teacher's program knowledge, know how, and problem solving skills to the point where the consultant need serve only as a resource for new ideas, new research, and as someone knowledgeable with whom to discuss new ideas.

Basic operating principles for the consultant

In using the interaction techniques within the framework of the change model, there remain several operating principles to be used when consulting with a teacher. Many of these principles seem self-evident when stated; unfortunately, they are easily forgotten when the consultants are involved in the complicated process of bringing about change. Consultants should:

1. *Make change the whole point of the relationship that is developing between the teacher and the consultant.* In many instances, these two individuals would not be work-

ing together or even know one another except for the purpose of change. The act of change should become a natural, normal part of the relationship.

2. *Begin change immediately.* Anxiety builds in the teacher who will be asked to change. The actual process of change is never as frightening as is its anticipation.

3. *Depend upon live observation.* One of the most important consultant skills is that of objective observing. Teachers are involved in the complicated task of teaching. Seldom do they have the time, nor have they been trained, to observe objectively their own students' behavior. Consequently, they are not necessarily good observers or good problem analyzers. It has been said that "A question well-stated is a question half-answered" (Isaac & Michael, 1981, p. 219). Teachers who know what the problem really is are well on the way to solving it. It is here, as an objective observer, that a consultant can most help a teacher.

4. *Avoid becoming evaluators.* This holds true whether it is an informally assumed role or a formal role assigned by the institution. It is extremely difficult, if not impossible, for teachers to develop open communication with someone who is responsible for evaluating and determining their future. This open communication is vital for a good relationship—one that produces positive change—but communication can be undermined by a consultant who brings to the relationship an attitude of evaluator and not helper.

5. *Maintain brief, objective notes on both observations and meetings.* These notes should not contain subjective or evaluative material, just a factual account that both teacher and consultant can use as a source of information. Any objectives, goals, or decisions made should be included.

6. *Use a team approach to the task.* The teacher and the consultant have the same long term goals. They are both working to help the students, they are both responsible for student learning, they solve problems together, and they

share ideas. Both people are essential to make the program work.

7. *Give the teacher as much decision making power as possible within the framework of the objectives.* When giving information in answer to a specific request (i.e., an idea for vocabulary development for low first grade students), the consultant should give more than one alternative, discuss all alternatives with the teacher, and have the teacher choose the one that best fits the needs of the situation.

8. *Focus on the teacher's strengths.* As with students, it is important for teachers to know what they are doing right. Therefore, the consultant may be the first person to give teachers recognition for their hard work and good ideas. Consultants who are former teachers should have an appreciation for the difficulty of the teaching process.

There are many more axioms of good consulting, such as carrying out promises made or keeping confidences, but these apply to all aspects of work life.

Summary

The combination of four aspects of KEEP may make it unique: the mandate to change the behavior of thousands of students; the bringing together of a multidisciplinary group of people with a long term commitment to look at a problem from different viewpoints in order to build a cohesive program; the development of a program that is not only a reading curriculum but a set of strategies for thinking, teaching, and interacting with students; and the dissemination of the program to schools with an accompanying permanent staff to train, support, and monitor the teachers using the program.

Although in some ways the institution and program may differ from some of the institutions and programs described in other chapters in this book, many of the problems encountered when trying to bring about change are similar. Most of the major problems arising from the changes required in this dissemination are related to the human factor. Although continually changing, an effective reading program was developed in six years. In the six years since, we have developed what we believe to be an effective model of change. In spite of this, we have been more successful at *alleviating* than *solving* problems. Personalities differ, situations differ, motivations differ. All of these affect the relationship between a consultant and a teacher.

From my perspective as one who nurtures change, all the effort, stress, and anxiety are worth it. All I have to do to convince myself of that is to return to one of the KEEP classrooms and experience the thrill of children learning and teachers caring.

References

Au, K.H., and Blake, K. *Implementation of the KEEP reading program, 1982-1983.* Technical Report No. 112. Honolulu, HI: Center for Development of Early Education, The Kamehameha Schools, 1984.

Au, K.H., and Hao, R.K. *A quality control system for reading instruction.* Technical Report No. 89. Honolulu, HI: Center for Development of Early Education, The Kamehameha Schools, 1983.

Bogert, K., Sloat, K.C.M., and Kent, M. *Training reading consultants: A description of the consultant training program at KEEP.* Honolulu, HI: Center for Development of Early Education, The Kamehameha Schools, in press.

Isaac, S., and Michael, W.B. *Handbook in research and evaluation.* San Diego, CA: Edits Publishers, 1981.

Jordan, C. The selection of culturally compatible teaching practices. *Educational Perspectives,* 1981, *20* (1), 16-19.

Pearson, P.D., and Johnson, D.D. *Teaching reading comprehension.* New York: Holt, Rinehart and Winston, 1978.

Shapiro, B., and Sloat, K.C.M. *The effect of role groups on a BARS development.* Technical Report No. 111. Honolulu, HI: Center for Development of Early Education, The Kamehameha Schools, 1984.

Tharp, R.G. The effective instruction of comprehension: Results and descriptions of the Kamehameha Early Education Program. *Reading Research Quarterly,* 1982, *17* (4), 503-527.

Tharp, R.G., and Gallimore, R. The regulatory function of teacher questions. Paper presented at the annual meeting of the National Reading Conference, Austin, Texas, December 1983.

Tharp, R.G., Jordan, C., Speidel, G.E., Au, K.H., Klein, T.W., Calkins, R.P., Sloat, K.C.M., and Gallimore, R. Product and process in applied developmental research: Education and the children of a minority. In M.E. Lamb, A.L. Brown, and B. Rogoff (Eds.), *Advances in developmental psychology,* volume 3. Hillsdale, NJ: Erlbaum, 1984.

Prelude

I n this chapter we get a different perspective on the process of change. The Graystone Project, developed by the teachers at Graystone School with the assistance of Robert Calfee, Marcia Henry, and Jean Funderburg, has the same underlying purpose as KEEP (described in Chapter 5): the improvement of student performance through the improvement of teaching strategies. But the underlying ethos and the operating procedures are quite different from those of KEEP. Both programs present teachers with generic strategies for modifying any lesson they might encounter, but the Graystone strategy is more curriculum focused compared with the more instruction focused strategy of KEEP. Calfee, Henry, and Funderburg try to convince teachers that this generic set of routines can turn an otherwise inglorious basal lesson into a masterpiece of curricular rationality. They sell their message quite well.

Robert Calfee
Marcia Henry
Jean Funderburg

6

A model for school change

Helping students become literate remains a fundamental challenge for American schools. Instruction in reading is the focus of the elementary school; between a third and a half of students' academic time during the first six years of schooling is spent on reading, spelling, and language arts, all of which are directed toward the acquisition of literacy.

Despite the efforts of a large corps of teachers and the mounting pressure from the public (both directly and as reflected in legislative and governmental agencies), after more than a decade of instruction, many youngsters leave school unable to read fluently and with insufficient understanding to meet the literacy demands of modern society. These deficiencies are not evident at lower levels of competence—the basic skills as measured by basic tests show signs of improvement on a yearly basis. The problem arises at the upper levels of performance—higher level skills such as comprehension have bumped along at an undesirably low level or declined over recent years (Copperman, 1978).

This chapter describes efforts to meet this challenge through Project READ, an ongoing, collaborative school improvement program involving several public schools in Northern California and a research team from Stanford University. The project was designed to help teachers learn to help their students acquire higher levels of reading skills. The primary aim of the project is to help students understand that both spoken and written language are tools for problem solving and communication.

If success in problem solving and communication is the ideal, what is the real world of classroom instruction in reading and language arts? Our observations and interviews suggest that most teachers go through the basal series unit by unit, relying on activities from the teacher's manual. As children read, they are interrupted frequently with literal questions from the teacher's edition. Scope and sequence charts display elaborate lists of instructional objectives, but rarely guide teachers in organizing material for their students. The manuals provide limited information about rationale and program goals. Teachers rely on workbooks and worksheets for practice in reading, with little classroom discussion or direct instruction in reading.

Other researchers have made similar observations. Osborn (1981), Rosecky (1978), and Shannon (1982) all found that teachers rely heavily on basal series and accompanying materials for reading programs. Chall (1983) questioned the early stress on silent reading and lamented the predominance of literal questions and the tendency, especially in the early grades, for directions and questions to distract children from the text. Weinstein (1982) noted that teachers rely on worksheets and workbooks that drill isolated skills. The benefits of small group discussion were discussed by Dillon (1981) and Johnson and Johnson (1981), but there is little evidence that this is common practice. Rosenshine (1981) found direct instruction lacking in reading groups; only 36 percent of reading instruction was teacher led in second grade, and the percentage was even lower in fifth grade.

In preliminary interviews, teachers in Project READ used a variety of terms to describe the focus of their reading instruction. These included *fluency, oral reading, silent reading, comprehension, literature, student enjoyment, phonics, reading mechanics,* and *sequencing.* None of the teachers described how these topics might relate to one another; the teachers seemed to lack a coherent model for thinking about reading instruction.

Project READ

Project READ is founded on the notion that the teacher with a well founded concept of reading and instruction will enhance student performance in problem solving and independent thinking as well as in test taking. We propose that teachers should be in charge of reading instruction; they should be able to analyze and to modify basal lessons as necessary.

Project READ does not call for a change in curriculum materials. The emphasis is on helping teachers use existing materials more effectively. All basal series have strengths and weaknesses—many contain interesting and well written texts, but most lack a coherent and explicit instructional plan for small group discussion. The project depends on well written texts, so if a series lacks appropriate materials teachers may need to search out supplementary texts. Some series are so strongly based in a particular instructional model that they cannot be adapted for use with Project READ. In most instances, however, a basal series provides sufficient materials for the project.

In Project READ, teachers are trained to analyze reading material critically so they will have a conceptual basis for selecting some materials, discarding others, and modifying many. This task can be demanding; we have found it helpful to provide support in materials analysis and to promote cooperative efforts among teachers so individuals are not left to bear the entire burden of planning and materials preparation.

The school as the locus of change

The design of Project READ assumes that significant changes in instructional practice must be initiated and sustained at the level of the local school. This assumption, which is consistent with the findings from research on effective schools (Edmonds, 1982), calls into question efforts to improve practice by working with individual teachers. One might question whether schools can be improved as a unit; sociologists describe schools as loosely coupled (Meyer & Rowan, 1977; Scott, 1981), meaning that teachers do what is expected of them without communicating with one another and without much guidance from the principal. We think two conditions are essential for school improvement, both of which have been incorporated into the design of the project.

The first condition is strong instructional leadership, generally by the principal. The role of the principal has grown over the past fifty years—schools are larger, demands for services are greater, and the margin for error is smaller. Principals often find themselves dividing their efforts among managing the school as a small business (or as a branch of a larger bureaucracy), maintaining relations with the client community, and providing instructional leadership (Blumberg & Greenfield, 1980; Calfee, 1981). While the instructional leadership role is often considered a vital responsibility, it is easily deferred to more pressing concerns, especially if the principal lacks training in curriculum and instruction. In any event, prior to implementing Project READ in a school, we attempt to ensure that the principal supports the program and is willing to go through the training program with members of the teaching staff.

The second condition for the attainment of a successful schoolwide program is the creation of a common conceptual framework. One reason for the decoupled character of a school may be the Babel like nature of present day training for elementary teachers. Most inservice programs focus attention on a single area of reading, and while they may shed some fresh ideas on the topic, the absence of an overarching framework means that the influence of such training on instructional practice is short lived. Lacking a common language, teachers spend little time talking about reading or instruction. A primary goal of Project READ is the acquisition by the school faculty of a robust concept of reading and instruction, which brings with it a shared language for communicating about these domains. For this reason, we devote considerable training to establishing a coherent theoretical base.

Theoretical framework

The theoretical framework for the project relies in part on research on human information processing over the past quarter century, which leads to the following characterization of the human mind (Calfee, 1981): Human beings are capable of remembering a great deal, but they have an extremely limited capacity to think about many different things at any one time. As a consequence of this limited capacity, information stored in the long term memory must be well organized. The mind tends naturally to organize repeated experiences; these naturally occurring schemata tend to be

Calfee, Henry, Funderburg

idiosyncratic to the individual, who is often unaware of the organization. Information also can be learned as a preorganized structure – much of what is presented as school knowledge has this character. For example, learning principles of Newtonian physics on the basis of natural experience is no easy matter, so the student is taught these principles as a way of (re)organizing experiences.

The fundamental principle in *In Search of Excellence* (Peters & Waterman, 1982) fits well with the nature of the human mind; knowledge and performance are enhanced to the degree that one observes KISS – "Keep It Simple, Stupid!" Simplicity is often found in a structure that possesses coherence; for our purposes, we have found it useful to define coherence as a system with a small number of distinctive elements (three to nine) bound together by one or two integrating themes.

The principle of coherence, represented by the notion of separable process models of human thinking (Calfee, 1981), has served as the foundation for developing models of the competent reader and the competent teacher. Not all readers and teachers operate according to our models, but to the extent that an individual's mental operations cannot be described by some coherent structure, it is likely that both knowledge and performance will suffer – or so the theory goes.

Model of reading

Reading appears on the surface to be a complex activity. The challenge for separable process theory is to discover a simple representation of these activities that can be used by teachers for instruction and by students for acquiring literacy. The separable process model portrays reading as a small number of distinctive elements that find their foundation in an analysis of the curriculum of reading (Figure 1).

Current instructional practice tends to braid all of these elements together in each lesson, with the result that neither teacher nor student gains a clear insight into the existence of the components as separate elements. Moreover, there is a tendency, because the separability is not appreciated, to neglect certain elements and overemphasize others. For example, vocabulary and decoding are often

Figure 1
Model of reading

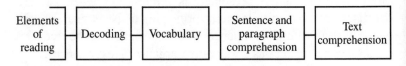

Decoding is the translation of print into some equivalent of speech.

Vocabulary is the assignment of meaning to words and the association of words and concepts within well ordered semantic spaces and taxonomies.

Sentence and paragraph analysis is the parsing of sentences, the analysis of inter-sentential relations, and the comprehension of a paragraph as an idea bearing unit.

Text comprehension is the selection of an overall thematic framework or skeleton for organizing an entire text.

confused in the minds of teachers, largely due to the way these components are presented in basals. Words that are unfamiliar and problematic for both decoding (word recognition) and vocabulary (meaning) are mixed in the vocabulary section preceding the reading of the text. By separating the elements conceptually, teachers gain a clearer understanding of the substance of each of these elements and can be more effective in analyzing student needs and the potential of curriculum materials for meeting needs in each of these domains.

Two themes play an important role in tying together these elements in reading instruction. One is the contrast between natural and formal language, the contrast between everyday experience and the content of schooling. This contrast can be used to enlighten each of the elements and to highlight the contribution of schooling to the development of language skills during childhood and adolescence.

The second theme comes from an examination of the history of the English language. English is a polyglot of several languages (most notably Anglo-Saxon and Romance). Analysis is critically important for understanding the apparent complexities of the written language; it also provides an insight into the dynamic character of language as an evolving representation of the culture.

Model of instruction

The complex task of instruction also can be represented as a relatively small number of separable components (Figure 2). This theoretical framework gives teachers a simple representation and a vocabulary for both reading and reading instruction.

Figure 2
Model of instruction

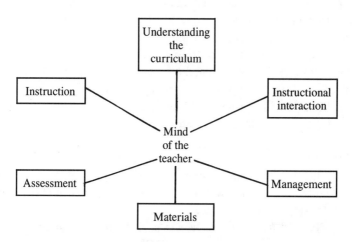

Understanding the curriculum is having a coherent representation of a domain such as reading or mathematics.

Instruction is having a model of learning (How do students learn? How does the teacher plan a lesson to best accommodate the nature of the learning process?).

Assessment is having a knowledge of the formal and informal methods of collecting evidence about a student's knowledge or level of skill.

Materials is being able to analyze critically the potential of a set of materials to attain an instructional goal and to identify the strengths and weaknesses of the materials.

Management is having strategies for managing people, time, space, and resources so instruction is conducted smoothly and appropriately.

Instructional interaction is following a set of principles for asking questions, giving feedback, praising, and guiding.

The practical side

The project stresses designing lessons as an exercise in small group problem solving. This theme is fundamental to an understanding of the scripts found in *The Book: Components of Reading Instruction* (Calfee & Associates, 1981-1984), an alternative to existing lesson plans. The scripts are designed to provide discussion models that can be used to enhance the effectiveness of existing materials.

Each script consists of a clear, simple opening statement that presents the purpose of the lesson in terms of its content, structure, and process. These same elements are stressed in the activities that make up the problem solving discussion and in the concluding statement in which students reflect on the substance and form of the lesson and on its meaning in other contexts. A script is a general purpose lesson frame, designed to focus on a well defined component of reading (decoding, vocabulary, or comprehension), but adaptable to a wide variety of content. *The Book* contains scripts on several activities within each of the major components.

• Decoding

The *Regular Short Words* script is designed to teach students to recognize common vowel and consonant patterns in short words of Anglo-Saxon origin.

The *Irregular Short Words* script provides strategies for learning common words that do not follow regular letter/sound correspondence (for example, *want, where, one,* and *only*).

The *Compound Words* script assists students in breaking compound words into their constituent words.

Structural Analysis for Decoding helps students decode polysyllabic words by breaking them into their morphological units — prefixes, roots, and suffixes.

• Vocabulary

Webbing facilitates teaching the concepts of word association and classification by helping students organize words and concepts in memory and by giving them a context for new vocabulary words.

Weaving is an extension of webbing for teaching vocabulary concepts; a collection of words is fashioned into an appropriate structure—often a matrix or hierarchy.

Words in Context encourages students to look for syntactic, associative, and referential cues in a passage to glean the meaning of the word.

Structural Analysis for Vocabulary teaches students the meanings of word elements such as prefixes, suffixes, and roots.

• Sentence and paragraph comprehension

The *Basic Sentence Frame* script introduces students to the most simple sentence patterns, while the *Phrase Modification* script makes students aware of the phrase relationships in a main clause.

The *Paragraph Signal Words* script helps students understand the elaborated relationships within a paragraph, while the *Paragraph Referents* script focuses on the pronoun reference relationship used between sentences within a paragraph.

• Text comprehension

The *Narrative* script provides a framework for analyzing the building blocks of a story, including characters, setting, time, episodes, and theme.

The *Expository Structure: Description* script facilitates teaching the structure and purpose of expository descriptive prose and focuses on the use of examples, definitions, facts, and other illustrative writing devices.

The *Expository Structure: Sequence* script helps students analyze expository prose that is organized according to a time ordered sequence.

The *Text Analysis* script provides students with strategies for analyzing the organization of a passage.

Implementation of the project

Project READ began in the summer of 1981 as a collaboration between the Stanford University School of Education and the faculty of Graystone Elementary School in San Jose, California. During the summer, a five day workshop was followed by preparation of *The Book*. The school year provided opportunities to give demonstration lessons, to observe, to hold one day workshops, and to refine techniques. The experiences left the project participants convinced that the basic approach had merit. By the summer of 1982, a cadre of graduate research assistants and school teachers were available as trainers. Graystone School provided a working model for the theoretical base where experienced READ teachers could give demonstration lessons and serve as small group discussion leaders for the workshops.

The introductory workshop

Participants begin with an intensive three day workshop that fulfills four objectives:

- The introduction and development of the theoretical foundations of the project, with emphasis on the separable process model of reading and instruction.
- An opportunity for teachers to use the theoretical framework to evaluate instructional materials from the basal series used at their schools.
- Discussion and demonstration of several scripts.
- Presentation of small group problem solving as an instructional method and opportunities for practice in small group discussion.

The first day begins with a demonstration of the instructional techniques, followed by an overview of the theoretical frameworks. Participants are introduced to scripted lessons and given *The Book*. On the second and third days, teachers apply the frameworks for critical analysis of instructional materials; each specific component is covered in more detail. For example, in decoding, there is a lecture on semantic fields and morphological structures. Teachers meet in small groups to discuss the presentation, to analyze a text, and to plan decoding instruction for the passage.

Postworkshop activities

Four sets of activities follow the workshops. First, project staff members visit the target schools during the fall to demonstrate sample scripts and to discuss with teachers their progress in applying the concepts and activities presented during the workshop.

Second, individual teachers are observed as they try out scripts in their classrooms. The objective is to give teachers prompt feedback on lesson content, structure, and process and to discuss their understanding of project techniques. To aid in scripting a specific lesson, project staff and participating teachers have devised microscripts and lesson critiques, minilessons that analyze the substance of a particular unit in a basal series and spell out some ideas about the format and small group discussion topics for the unit. They serve both as a time saving device and as a model of the process.

Third, two or three sessions, held at individual schools, lead the teaching staff through an evaluation of their progress in the program and provide an opportunity for introducing additional scripts.

At the end of the school year, the teachers are interviewed about their overall concept of reading and instruction and their thoughts about the impact of the project on their teaching and on the school's reading program. Their goals are more articulate teachers; greater reliance on small group discussion effective for their students; and integration of reading with the related language arts of writing, spelling, grammar, and speaking.

Planning and conducting the lesson

A traditional basal lesson presents five to ten vocabulary words to read aloud and to define, sometimes by using a glossary or a dictionary, sometimes by using context. Students then are asked a motivating question related to the text. Students read the text, interrupted by occasional questions at various points in the story. Student discussion is guided at the end of the reading by a list of questions. The lesson concludes with seatwork from the basal workbook. More challenging activities may be found in a concluding enrichment section, but few teachers find time for these activities. The teacher's manual provides specific guidance on many points, but not on the critical issues of time allocation, adapting to different ability levels, or class management.

In Project READ, the goal of analysis of a basal lesson is to determine the most appropriate activities—direct instruction, discussion, independent work—for a given situation. What is appropriate will depend on the skills and abilities of the students as well as the content of the specific text. Thoughtful consideration of the text itself, the information in the teacher's edition, the teacher's knowledge of theoretical concepts, and the students' strengths and weaknesses are the basic ingredients for successful lesson planning. In essence, the teacher's edition becomes one of many tools available for the development of high quality lessons.

Planning. To begin, the teacher does an overview of the unit, scanning quickly to provide a background and indicate the elements of emphasis in the unit. The teacher should look for opportunities to develop scripts in any of the major components—decoding, vocabulary, and comprehension. The range of student needs is also considered during the analysis.

The teacher then reads the passage twice, once for interest and the second time for focus, keeping in mind the basic components. Length and quality of the text should be noted, as they will determine the number of lessons. If the text provides several opportunities to develop scripts in one or more of the components, more class time should be spent on the text than if it has less potential for script development. It is not necessary to devote the same amount of class time to each text. Indeed, texts of little interest might be skipped.

The passage type must be determined. Is the text narrative or expository? The passage is narrative if it contains a setting and has character development, a plot, a problem and resolution, and a sequence of events or episodes. The passage is expository if it describes an event, person, or thing; presents a logical time sequence for a factual event or gives a logical set of directions or steps; and makes an argument or attempts to persuade.

Some passages mix narration and exposition. The teacher then has to decide on which portion to focus during the lesson or how to handle the more difficult task of text analysis. What is the most important aspect of the passage? What should the students remember from the passage?

The analysis contains a few more steps. Review the teacher's manual; go to the front of the text and read the background summary and other suggestions for possible information and ideas. Go

Calfee, Henry, Funderburg

to the back of the text for followup activities, information, and ideas. Be sure to check the Enrichment section.

Once the story is familiar, the type has been determined, and varied suggestions from the teacher's manual have been digested, it is time to decide on reading components for script development — one, several, or none.

Decoding. Look at the unit overview to see when specific skills are introduced, reinforced, and practiced. There are often too many skills in one lesson to teach realistically. By reorganizing the unit, most skills can be taught in a more rational, logical order. Often worksheets and lessons from various stories can be combined to prepare a successful lesson. Perhaps several words used in a passage follow a similar pattern. These may be used in a decoding lesson, even though this has not been suggested.

Vocabulary. Consider the vocabulary of the story. Is there a set of related words or concepts that could be associated in a semantic network or web? Words with prefixes and suffixes may fit nicely into a structural analysis script. It is not necessary to introduce the vocabulary exactly as it is presented in the teachers' edition. Patterns in words and the interrelatedness of words are more important than memorizing a list of randomly associated words. It is not necessary to introduce all unfamiliar words to the students before reading a story. Students pick up the meaning in context. If a word is critical to a story, it may be most efficient to tell students what the word means and how it is pronounced.

Comprehension: Narrative. Determine the passage type, then decide if there are elements of story structure that should be emphasized in a lesson. To do this, consider these elements: setting, character development, episode identification, episode analysis (problem, response, outcome, action), story graph development, and theme/main idea identification. Identify the clearest and most important aspect of the passage, which will become the focus for the discussion during the comprehension script. If more than one element appears important for discussion in a lesson, other middle activities can be included in the script or additional scripts can be planned.

Comprehension: Expository. If the passage describes an event, person, or thing, a descriptive script is appropriate. When the passage presents a logical time sequence or a logical set of directions or steps, a sequential script should be used. Expository texts in basal series are often mixtures of sequence and description, in which case teacher judgment is essential.

Teaching the lesson

To demonstrate how the process works, we will go through a possible lesson, showing how a Project READ teacher plans instruction. "Trail Boss" from the Ginn Reading Program (1982), Level 13, Grade 6, tells about a twelve year old girl's confrontations as she takes her family's herd of longhorn cattle from Texas to Illinois. The text is well suited for a text comprehension lesson on plot analysis with possibilities for a decoding lesson on compound words and a vocabulary lesson leading to a followup writing activity. The project method calls for each of these components to be the focus of a separate lesson. These are sketched in the following sections.

• Comprehension

After the teacher determines the text is narrative, she or he must decide which elements of narrative structure to emphasize. In introducing the lesson, teacher and students might discuss how stories are constructed and point out some of the building blocks such as setting, character, events, episodes, or theme.

"Trail Boss" is ideal for discussing story episodes and drawing a story graph to highlight the sequence of events. The story consists of two basic episodes. The first concerns Emma Jane's encounter with a Missouri farmer, while the second focuses on her attempt to cross a guarded bridge with her herd of cattle. The episodic analysis fits a common pattern (see Figure 3).

Teachers occasionally have different labels for the terms used in Figure 3 (problem/initiating event, response/reaction, action/attempt, and outcome/resolution); terminology is less important than the structural concepts. Terms will vary depending on the taxonomy used in the basal or in prior instruction.

Calfee, Henry, Funderburg

Figure 3
Pattern for "Trail Boss" episodes

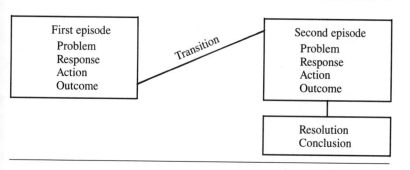

As the group discusses how episodes fit together to make up a story, a story graph can be used to document the story plan. Students construct a story line and label events within each episode. Students reflect on the sequence of events, the high point of the story, and events leading to the high point, then mark the events on a continuum ranging from tense to calm (see Figure 4). Students are asked to provide the rationale for the sequence and may be challenged by classmates. Students may find evidence for their choices from the text, especially when disagreements arise.

The closing of the lesson should focus on content ("Trail Boss"), structure (episodes and sequence), and process (plot analysis and story graph). The students may summarize or retell the story using their story graph as a basis. Closings are seldom provided in the basal, but seem an important step in reviewing what has been learned and how this learning might be used in other situations.

Although the story ends with the cattle safely across the bridge, one can imagine subsequent events. As a followup activity, students could write a final episode. They would review the pattern of most episodes before writing their composition. Transfer of the process to new material is one of the major goals of the scripted lessons.

Figure 4
Story graph

	Calm	Tense

First episode

> *Setting:* Emma talks to stranger about crossing his land with her herd
>
> *Problem:* "Not across my land you're not"
>
> *Response:* "They won't do harm unless you stampede them"
>
> *Action:* "I'll settle this with your Pa!" "Pa's dead"
>
> *Outcome:* "You can cross my land but watch out for the bridge at Clinton"

Transition

> "I'll outmaneuver them"

Second episode

> *Problem:* There are men at the bridge
>
> *Response:* Emma and her brother plan to cross after dark
>
> *Action:* As they lead cattle to the bridge, a man shouts
>
> *Outcome:* Cattle stampede
>
> *Resolution:* Cattle slow down as rider yells "Turn them left"

Final resolution

> They discover who the rider is and how he helped

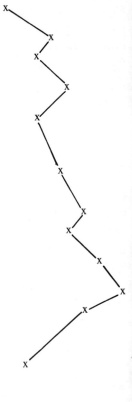

• Decoding

"Trail Boss" contains a large number of colorful compound words. It gives the teacher an opportunity to review one of the major ways by which English words are created—compounding—and to contrast this approach with the other major technique—affixation.

Calfee, Henry, Funderburg

Decoding and meaning overlap in this area; compounding helps the student in pronouncing a long word and in understanding a complex and possibly unfamiliar word. The lesson can be organized to focus exclusively on decoding or on vocabulary or on both. The teacher may point out that knowing the meaning of both small words may assist in understanding the compound word, e.g., *longhorns* and *canebrakes*.

Lists of compound words from the story are written on the board.

firelight	moonlight	longhorns	pigtailed
hoofbeats	greenhorn	canebrakes	everything
toylike	countryside	eyebrows	
horseman	sundown	outfit	

The teacher begins the discussion by probing with questions: "How are these words alike?" "What small words are inside each long word?" "How are the words different?" "What kind of words are these?" "How do you know?" Students read the words individually or as a group and may be asked to generate other compound words to add to the list. Then the teacher may dictate compound words for spelling.

In closing the lesson, the teacher asks the students to summarize the content (compound words), the process (identify the individual words), structure (big words composed of two smaller words), and goal of the lesson (to make compound words easier to decode or to understand).

Followup activities should encourage generalization of the strategy to new materials. Students may divide compound words they find in their reading or use compound words in stories.

• Vocabulary

Although a vocabulary lesson may be taught before students read a story, words from "Trail Boss" provide an excellent motivation for a followup writing activity. The teacher generates a list of pertinent words from the text related to several categories and puts the category labels on the blackboard. To stimulate the discussion, the teacher asks, "In which category does this word belong?" (see Figure 5).

Figure 5
Word bank for composition based on "Trail Boss"

Emma Jane	Cattle	Horses	The man	Areas
spunky	trample	buck	nasal twang	bluff
stubborn	stampede	gallop	hostile eyes	valley
determined	plod	rear	curt voice	range
outmaneuvering	bellow	hooves	gray brows	ridge
calm	balk		leathery face	hollow
drover	longhorn			bridge
	steer			canebrakes

Evaluation

Although Project READ has been implemented in more than a dozen schools, it is still evolving. We have built in a continuous evaluation plan, and we modify the project according to the feedback we receive. A variety of sources provides information. For example, workshop evaluations have prompted some modifications. Teachers respond that they are overwhelmed and somewhat confused by the amount of information presented the first day. In contrast, at the end of the third day there is a dramatic shift in the evaluations; teachers are challenged and anxious to use the strategies they have learned.

End of year evaluations show us that teachers require planning to implement the project in their classroom, not only in terms of content but because it relies on student participation. Teachers report students are better at using formal language in both speaking and writing. In schools where the project has been implemented by most of the teachers, standardized test scores have gone up by one-half to one full grade level equivalent.

The separable process concepts provide a foundation and the scripts a practical vehicle for making teachers more articulate about reading instruction. Teachers grasp the idea of the four component model of reading with little difficulty; are able to identify specific components in their basal lessons; and, with practice, can modify instruction to focus on one component at a time.

In addition, teachers gain expertise in critically evaluating the basal passages and begin to expand the level of questions; to provide

Calfee, Henry, Funderburg

more enrichment activities; and to encourage followup activities, usually in the area of writing. They are more cautious about omitting basal objectives or modifying the sequence of presentation.

There are hurdles to implementation of the project. The script format is new to teachers and additional preparation time is needed. Teachers need support during the first year until the method becomes automatic. The process works more smoothly when the principal provides leadership for the project.

The project has influenced teacher attitudes and morale. Teachers report the project provides a set of conceptual and practical tools that allow them to take an active role in implementing a coherent, stimulating, and efficacious program of instruction in literacy. Teachers have a sense of professional competence, control, and self awareness. They share a common language and framework to discuss reading instruction. They discuss the reading curriculum across grade levels and value a new sense of professional camaraderie.

Teachers and students alike enjoy the greater amount of classroom discussion. Both are actively involved in the learning process by their increased participation. Teachers and parents are pleased with the increased quality and quantity of children's writing. The composition by a first grader shown in Figure 6 reflects not only rich vocabulary but an understanding of episodic structure. Sean's teacher introduced the writing assignment by having students web on the word *treasure*. Sean selected words from the web as the basis for his composition.

A variety of activities helps sustain the project. Impromptu working sessions at the school give teachers an opportunity to discuss and develop new lessons and to review the theoretical framework. A monthly newsletter keeps teachers informed about project events. Project members are assigned to local schools as liaisons, providing a link between the university and the school site.

The primary foundation for the project is normative; we think that the principles have a strong grounding in scholarship. An empirical base of support is being compiled, with results to date supportive though not definitive.

Figure 6
Composition by Sean, grade one

Finding Treasures

Sean

Me and my crew went underwater to look for treasures. We had to use some tools and a map, shovels, air tanks, mask, swimming suit, flippers too. We found the treasure at last and we opened it. There was gold and diamonds too. Then some pirates came they tried to get the gold. Bot they didn't get it. then we ad to leav now.

Calfee, Henry, Funderburg

References

Blumberg, A., and Greenfield, W. *The effective principal.* Boston, MA: Allyn & Bacon, 1980.

Calfee, R.C. Cognitive psychology and educational practice. In D.C. Berliner (Ed.), *Review of research in education.* Washington, DC: American Educational Research Association, 1981, 3-73.

Calfee, R.C., and Associates. *The Book: Components of reading instruction.* (A generic manual for reading teachers.) Unpublished manuscript, Stanford University, 1981-1984.

Chall, J.S. *Learning to read: The great debate,* revision. New York: McGraw-Hill, 1983.

Copperman, P. *The literacy hoax.* New York: William Morrow, 1978.

Dillon, D. Editor's page. *Language Arts,* 1981, *60,* 955.

Edmonds, R.R. Programs of school improvement: An overview. *Educational Leadership,* 1982, *40,* 4-11.

Ginn Reading Program. *Flights of color,* teacher's edition. Lexington, MA: Ginn, 1982.

Johnson, D.W., and Johnson, F.P. *Joining together,* second edition. Englewood Cliffs, NJ: Prentice-Hall, 1981.

Meyer, J.W., and Rowan, R. Institutionalized organizations: Formal structures as myth and ceremony. *American Journal of Sociology,* 1977, *83,* 340-363.

Osborn, J. *The purposes, uses, and contents of workbooks and some guidelines for teachers and publishers.* Report No. 27. Champaign, IL: Center for the Study of Reading, University of Illinois, 1981.

Peters, T.J., and Waterman. R.H. *In search of excellence.* New York: Harper & Row, 1982.

Rosecky, M. Are teachers selective when using basal guidebooks? *The Reading Teacher,* 1978, *31,* 381-384.

Rosenshine, B.V. How time is spent in elementary classrooms. *Journal of Classroom Interaction,* 1981, *17,* 16-25.

Scott, R. *Organizations: Rational, natural, and open systems.* Englewood Cliffs, NJ: Prentice-Hall, 1981.

Shannon, P. Some subjective evidence for teachers' reliance on commercial reading materials. *The Reading Teacher,* 1982, *35,* 884-889.

Weinstein, R. Comprehension is the key: Reading center finds the way to help. *APA Monitor,* 1982, *13,* 37.

Prelude

I rene Gaskins is the founder and guiding light of Benchmark School in Media, Pennsylvania. As you read about Benchmark, the ideas, methods, teaching strategies, and enthusiasm of the place seem almost to jump off the page. What you find at Benchmark is dedicated teachers who have made a commitment to working with students who have problems learning many things, including reading. You also find an excellent program designed to promote professional growth and development. Gaskins begins with the philosophy that pervades professional staff development at Benchmark; then presents a series of mini-case studies to illustrate problems and solutions; and, finally, offers a set of principles to ponder as you try to solve similar problems on your own. The tension between directed development and mutual adaptation in change efforts underlies much of what happens at Benchmark.

7

Irene W. Gaskins

Helping teachers adapt to the needs of students with learning problems

A generation of children has passed through school since I first accepted the challenge of helping teachers adapt their reading programs to the needs of their students. In the intervening years I have discovered no panacea for effecting change; however, I have learned some basic factors related to success in implementing change that would have made my earlier attempts easier.

In those early years as a district reading consultant I continually felt as if I were up against a wall of resistance. Teachers either seemed afraid to change or were genuinely convinced of the merits of the program in use. Their resistance to change was not totally unfounded, for the majority of their students were making satisfactory progress in reading.

My concern was for the few students in each class who were not succeeding. Remedial reading classes several times a week were not the answer, perhaps because they offered more of the same approach that had not worked in the first place. Even when the remedial class included methods tailored to each child's learning style, the students did not catch up to grade level in reading. The students needed more than could be accomplished in a short remedial period several times a week. A full day of instruction matched to individual styles of learning would have been ideal, yet the majority of each student's school day was spent in a classroom where teachers taught as if everyone in the class learned the same way. Few if any adaptations were made to unique learning styles. As a result of these experiences, I could not help but wonder what the effect would have been on the success of these underachievers had the teachers believed it was they who needed to adapt to the students rather than vice versa.

Wanting to test the hypothesis that poor readers would have a better chance for success if teachers adapted to individual student learning styles, and having the support of a group of dedicated professionals and parents, in 1970 I opened a private, ungraded school for bright poor readers—Benchmark School. A few key beliefs and values, such as "All I can change is me," "Every child can learn to read," and "There is no best method," were set down as the cornerstones of the school's program. Within these beliefs and values, innovation, experimentation, and adaptations were encouraged.

This chapter tells the story of how teachers at Benchmark School are supported and guided in their efforts to adapt to the needs of our 150 students, ages six to fourteen, who have learning problems. The first section gives an overview of the kinds of changes that have taken place at Benchmark. Following this, I describe four characteristics that have fostered an environment for change. In the last section, I discuss some problems we have encountered in implementing change as well as the solutions that seemed to work.

Benchmark: A case study in change

In Fall 1970 seventeen intellectually bright poor readers entered Benchmark School and our teachers began the process of adapting to meet children's needs. We had no choice but to adapt programs and to be innovative. Our seventeen children had already proved that traditional programs did not work for them. Teachers did the changing. They kept their methodologies flexible, shifting from one to another as necessary, rather than expecting the students to fit the teachers' favorite techniques and methods. We thought we held the secret to success.

Change in classroom management and instruction

We were not in session long before a concern arose about how to keep students on task and behaving appropriately. Our belief had been that any behavior problems exhibited prior to Benchmark were related to lack of success in reading; thus behavior would improve

Gaskins

when students were given appropriate instruction and allowed to succeed. However, we learned that there was more to effective instruction than better reading methods. In search of answers to our concerns about on task behavior, we consulted with teachers and psychologists and surveyed the special education literature.

We soon realized that we had to do a lot of changing if we were going to succeed in teaching these children how to read. The alternative to our changing was to place the responsibility for change on the students or their parents, yet we were convinced that all we could change was ourselves, and so we did. First, we altered the difficulty level of independent work: Seatwork was made easier and given in smaller doses so students experienced almost 100 percent success. Second, we instituted reward systems: Tokens were given to students at frequent intervals for achieving such goals as staying in their seats, raising their hands for assistance, or keeping their eyes on the speaker. Books read and worksheets completed were entered on charts and students worked together to earn class parties or extra recess time. And these changes helped: On task time and behavior improved, and so did the students' reading ability.

Our first major changes were implemented more quickly than others would be. We viewed appropriate student behavior as a prerequisite to teaching these children to read. Sometimes other concerns, such as an improved writing or word identification program, would not seem as crucial as appropriate student behavior; thus change would not occur as easily or as quickly. At other times, especially in our early years, we found that the need for change had to be addressed by broadening the curriculum rather than expecting teachers to change.

For example, the quality of mathematics and handwriting instruction suffered during our first two years because teachers were putting all their energy into doing what they knew and did best and what they felt the children needed most—reading instruction. Expecting teachers to put additional time into planning, especially in areas with which they were not familiar due to their reading specialist backgrounds, seemed unrealistic. Two former teachers who were volunteer aides at the school noticed our lopsided curriculum and each offered to assume responsibility for one of these programs.

Thus mathematics, an area of success for many of our students, and handwriting, a frequent area of weakness, became regularly scheduled parts of each child's program. These skills were taught by teachers who could devote full preparation time to a high quality of instruction in their designated areas.

Change in the writing program

Much of the impetus for the curriculum changes at Benchmark has come from the followup evaluation we conduct for our graduates when they leave us and return to public or private schools. For example, some years ago we noted on questionnaires returned by teachers of our graduates that the quality of the graduates' written composition was generally rated as much poorer than their reading ability. Our placement counselor, who coordinates placement and followup of graduates, shared this concern with the staff. We searched the professional literature for direction in improving our writing program and invited an expert to present to us recommendations on how to get started.

As a result, a new writing program was born. The first year, a process approach to writing was piloted in one classroom. The improvement in the students' writing and reading was amazing, a fact that did not go unnoticed the next year among the teachers whose classes included the graduates of this pilot class. Benchmark teachers began to ask the pilot teacher to do demonstration composition lessons in their classrooms. They also observed the pilot teacher in her own classroom. The third year the pilot teacher became a full time supervisor and spent more time doing demonstration lessons and guiding the implementation of the writing program.

Five years later, the effectiveness of the writing program still varied among the fourteen classrooms. Supervisors still found the need to guide and support the teachers in implementing the program. All classroom teachers seemed to agree on the value of the program and all devoted thirty to forty-five minutes a day to helping their students learn to write, write to communicate, or write to enhance learning in other subjects (such as writing summaries or taking notes). However, the amount of time devoted to various aspects of the program—such as teacher comments written on papers, individual teacher-student conferences, or the degree of emphasis on content, organization, clarity, and mechanics—differed from classroom to classroom. Because we believed there was no one right way to teach writing, this variation among teachers was inevitable.

The new writing program was slower to take hold schoolwide than other curriculum innovations. The reluctance to try the program seems in part to have been due to the fact that the methods and priorities of a process approach to writing, which entailed allowing children to write on self selected topics and required teachers to teach to the needs exhibited by that writing, are the antithesis of the writing programs the teachers had been using previously. In addition, the teachers were concerned about whether a process approach to writing would prepare our graduates to fit into public and private school writing programs that were more traditional and textbook oriented than ours. Now that we have feedback that our graduates are doing well in writing, the process approach is widely accepted at Benchmark.

Change in seatwork and level of material for instruction

Change at Benchmark takes place not only with respect to major curriculum revision, as has occurred in written composition, but also in instructional practices as discussed earlier with respect to increasing student time on task and on decreasing behavioral problems. A third type of change that occurs at Benchmark is change in policies.

A few years ago, we observed that students who read the most books seemed to make the most progress. This observation was bolstered by confirmation from the literature and from our inservice speakers. Hence we formed a new policy regarding seatwork. At a full staff meeting, the teachers agreed that the policy regarding seatwork should be that each student be given the opportunity daily to read as much as possible at his/her independent (easy) level and to make some brief response to that reading. This brought about a dramatic and immediate change in seatwork. Workbooks were replaced with trade books. Worksheets with many questions per story or chapter were changed to include only one or two all encompassing questions. These changes literally took place overnight in most classrooms.

Another example of policy change has to do with reading level. Again, the impetus for the new policy came from our own observation about what seemed to work best for our students plus the confirmation of that observation from the professional literature and inservice speakers. We established a policy that students should continue at an instructional level until they read with the fluency and comprehension one would expect of students at their independent level. Although most teachers have discovered that keeping students at so called easy levels does not lessen achievement gains during a year, some still find it difficult to carry out this policy. One reason for their reluctance is their desire to share the excitement and sense of gratification students feel when they move to higher levels. A second reason is the pressure parents exert on teachers to place their children in higher level material.

Change in schoolwide goals

The times when change has seemed most difficult at Benchmark often have been when priorities were not clear. Poorly defined priorities seem to make change even more risky and threatening than usual. Therefore, we try to keep open lines of communication among the staff in order to assess and revise school priorities more effectively. For example, several years ago we set as a priority that students should be provided with the opportunity to make one and a half years of progress each year in reading level. Recently, teachers have noticed among students who had been at Benchmark several years that some of the strongest readers are those who spent the most time being instructed at "comfortable" levels, levels that some might call their independent levels. The priority of making one and a half years of progress each year has been changed to lessen the pressure on teachers to move students too quickly from level to level. The goal now reads "to give children the opportunity to experience what it is like to read like a good reader reads."

Whether change has to do with curriculum, instructional practices, policies, or priorities, it comes in many sizes and at many rates. We have discovered that change is necessary both on a daily basis, such as meeting a student's immediate instructional need, and over time, such as changing a broad curriculum policy. Exemplary instruction emerges only when administrators, supervisors, and teachers are receptive to change. The remainder of this chapter discusses the process of change at Benchmark—our successes and our problems.

Four characteristics of an environment for change

Looking back over the past seventeen years, it appears that at least four factors have contributed significantly to the Benchmark staff's success in adapting to the needs of poor readers: climate, involvement, ownership, and knowledge. These characteristics developed, not because of shrewd planning on my part, but because I set out to create the kind of school in which I would enjoy working.

Climate

While working in various teaching and consulting positions I became aware that the propensity to change is highly related to a school's climate or ambience. At Benchmark we soon confirmed this. By creating a climate in which the staff received satisfaction and felt safe, we seemed to increase the likelihood that teachers would take the risks necessary to change. A sense of excitement, high expectations, trust, and administrative responsiveness to staff needs are characteristics that have contributed to a satisfying and safe climate at Benchmark.

From the day the school started there has been a sense of excitement about working at Benchmark—a feeling of being pioneers in an unexplored land. Because we believe there is no one right way to teach reading, staff members have always been free to be innovative in their search for the best student method match. Teachers seem to find it exciting to teach in a climate where searching for a better way is the norm and taking a risk is applauded and supported.

A second important feature of the climate is high expectations. Through a careful selection process, which usually includes the requirement of an internship at Benchmark, we have been able to choose and train an exceptionally gifted group of teachers—the best available. This selection process begins the cycle of knowing we have the best, being able to expect the best, getting the best, and reinforcing that expectation of quality. In addition, teachers expect to be continually evaluating and adapting their methods. Benchmark teachers do not feel they have learned all there is to know. Because teachers have observed that teaching at Benchmark occurs in an atmosphere of love and concern for individual students and their families, they would not expect to act in any other way.

Third, the climate is characterized by trust. Teachers know they are hired because they bring special abilities, talents, and knowledge to the staff. When teachers are hired, we stress that professional growth is ongoing and that undoubtedly they will discover areas of relative weakness in their repertoire of skills in which they will want to grow professionally. Knowing that their numerous strengths are valued and respected, yet expecting that everyone on the staff wants to grow professionally, teachers seem to feel comfortable in revealing concerns and seeking assistance regarding their inadequacies, uncertainties, and questions. The supervisory staff takes care to accentuate the positive, to individualize supervision according to the teacher's stage of commitment and development, and to reinforce teachers for seeking guidance from them or other staff members. An environment of trust is established by our beliefs that all teachers intend to give each student the very best instruction they can and that any shortcoming is due only to lack of knowledge about how to meet a specific need.

A fourth factor that seems important in creating a satisfactory school climate is administrative responsiveness to staff needs. In all that is said and done, the administrative and supervisory staff tries to convey the message that people are important. To accomplish this, we feel administrators and supervisors need to be readily accessible to the staff. Accessibility has been accomplished at Benchmark through an open door, sign up policy and by making sure that administrative/supervisory staff systematically moves through the school each day to interact with the staff. The key in both instances is listening. Administrators and supervisors ask teachers for their opinions on particular situations as well as how they feel things are going in their classrooms. They take action to meet staff needs where possible and share with the staff any problems they may encounter in responding to staff needs. It is important that staff members feel their input has been given fair consideration. In early June of each year, a meeting is held where staff members meet in small groups to give input about things they would like to see changed at Benchmark. Staff input is recorded and categorized; then the administrator and supervisors hold an all day meeting to plan ways to respond to the staff's input. As a result of this process, numerous changes are made each year.

Involvement

During the first year of Benchmark School, the staff had little choice but to be involved. I needed and valued their input then, and this need continues to the present. In those early days in the school's history, the entire staff met around my desk one afternoon a week in what were almost always problem solving sessions. Later the aides would monitor or teach classes for the teachers while we met on Friday afternoons. Today, with a staff of over sixty, involvement is fostered in many ways: Teachers and psychologists meet individually each week with their supervisors; the faculty interacts at monthly staff meetings and weekly coordinators' meetings; aides meet monthly with their coordinator and daily with their teachers; staff members respond to questionnaires; and staff members have their input discussed at weekly supervisors' meetings. The meetings and questionnaires are used to identify problems, gather data, discuss ideas, formulate solutions, and monitor progress.

Although a problem solving approach is predominant, administrators and supervisors do not solve the problems. Instead, they involve staff members in problem solving discussions, often acting as sounding boards while the staff members generate alternative ideas and decide on a plan of action. We have learned that the likelihood of a teacher adapting or making changes to better meet the needs of students is much greater if the change is the staff member's idea than if it seems to have been dictated by the supervisor.

Schoolwide changes in curriculum and instruction evolve constantly at Benchmark because staff members have identified the need for change and have been part of the research, field testing, and final decision to implement. Teachers are encouraged to read, think, and talk about new and possibly better ways of teaching students. Renewal is through staff involvement.

Ownership

Involvement in problem solving almost always spawns a variety of possible solutions. At Benchmark School, the staff is encouraged and supported in testing these solutions, and this process seems to result in a commitment to developing a method that works. Arriving at the conclusion on one's own that a particular solution, method, or technique is best in a particular situation creates ownership. Being told that "This is the way we've always done it" or "Try this, it has worked for everyone else" not only deprives a teacher of the satisfaction of ownership, but often creates resentment.

Sources for the ideas our teachers own are numerous. The idea may be totally original with the teacher, adapted from another source, or used exactly as someone else developed it. For example, as a result of having observed another teacher teach or having heard a teacher talk about a particular method or technique, a teacher may implement or adapt an idea. If the idea works and it becomes part of the classroom routine, the teacher has taken ownership of the idea. The key is that the teacher who owns an idea has made the decision to accept the idea; it was not imposed on him/her.

Champions of new ideas are encouraged in a number of ways. Teachers have the autonomy to test their ideas systematically. They may present their new practices to the entire staff in a regularly scheduled forum. They also have a mentor and coach at their disposal.

During the development and field testing of a new practice, supervisors act as mentors and coaches. The stage is set for innovation and adaptation to meet student needs by the supervisors, who encourage their teachers to be open about concerns. The pervasive, supportive, nonthreatening climate makes it comfortable for teachers to discuss classroom problems. It is important that the problem to be solved originate with the teacher rather than the supervisor, though supervisors might guide a teacher to discover a problem. The supervisor and teacher research and discuss possible solutions together, but it is the teacher who decides on the solution to be tried, thus making a personal investment that helps to ensure the success of the proposed change. As the teacher begins to field test the new practice, the supervisor observes, gives feedback, acts as a trouble shooter and sounding board, and, where appropriate, creates enthusiasm for the new practice among the staff; however it is always the teacher who owns the idea. The teacher or the supervisor always conducts some kind of pre and posttesting in order to evaluate the new practice.

As it becomes evident that the new practice is working well to meet specific kinds of needs, the supervisor arranges for the teacher to share the details of the new practice with the rest of the staff. The staff is free to reject, use, or adapt the new idea. Because we trust the staff to do what is in the best interest of their students, we rarely feel the need to dictate that a new practice be implemented. We have learned that if the teacher is not convinced a method or technique will work, it probably will not. Ownership greatly enhances the likelihood that a new practice will be successful.

Knowledge

What is the source of the seemingly endless ideas for innovation, experimentation, and adaptation? Some of the ideas originate with individual teachers or supervisors. Most result from the staff's knowledge of what is happening in the field. Professional growth was a common interest of the original Benchmark staff, and we try hard to perpetuate that value.

Benchmark's professional library is extensive and well used. Each year the school subscribes to over twenty-five professional journals. Interested staff members register with the librarian to receive new issues of the journals they are interested in reading. Signing up is purely voluntary. Each journal is read by at least one person. Journals directly related to the primary needs of our population, such as *The Reading Teacher* and *Language Arts,* are more widely read. Journal readers often underline points of interest or write notes in the margins and then pass the journal to someone who would be particularly interested in the articles.

In addition to journals, the professional library contains reports from various research centers. Just as research reports are continually being added to the professional library, professional book reviews are perused and books that appear to be relevant to teaching at Benchmark are ordered. Each research report and professional book is reviewed by someone on the staff and shared with those who have expressed interest in the topics covered.

For years, Benchmark teachers and supervisors have met weekly after school for what has become known as a research seminar. There is a core group of six to eight teachers and supervisors who always attend the seminar, and eight to ten additional staff members who attend depending on their interest in the topic being discussed. The person in charge of the seminar for a particular week combs the library for articles and books related to a particular topic, and these are shared with interested seminar members, each of whom picks one to report on at the research seminar. The rules in reporting are to summarize briefly, evaluate the article, and spend the remainder of the time leading a discussion on "What does this have to do with teaching at Benchmark?" Sparks seem to fill the air at meetings where applications to practice are discussed and developed.

Professional reading keeps us abreast of who is doing exciting things in the field. Each month one of these experts is invited to Benchmark to present a day of inservice. Interacting with these researchers and innovators is a stimulating experience. Usually, each staff member leaves the inservice with at least one idea for a change to make in working with students. In some cases, a process of curriculum change is initiated that goes on for years and requires the expert to return several times to suggest ideas for revising and moving ahead.

Attendance at professional conferences is supported by the school. Staff members who attend summarize what they have gained from the conference and distribute copies to the staff. Often a special meeting is called to allow staff members to ask clarifying questions about the ideas presented at the conference.

Teachers are encouraged to submit proposals for making presentations at local, state, and national conferences. We have found that the need to research and organize ideas clearly enough to present them outside Benchmark has benefits for the Benchmark staff as well.

Writing for publication is also encouraged. The staff's writing of *Teaching for Success: Administrative and Classroom Practices at*

Benchmark School (Gaskins & Elliot, 1983) provided us with unexpected benefits in professional growth. Staff members felt a need to verify the validity of their ideas through a literature search and to become much more specific and clear in their presentation than they had felt a need to be when implementing the practices in their classrooms. As a result of the process of writing about what we did, our programs became more consistent and systematic.

Recently, coordinators have been appointed to spearhead staff development in specific areas. At an end of the year school evaluation meeting, the staff expressed a desire for more help in developing three specific curriculum areas: word identification/spelling, reading in the content areas, and metacognition. A coordinator was appointed for each area. During the summer, the three coordinators researched their areas and in the fall began to apply and share their findings. They tried out ideas in their classrooms, shared articles and teaching materials, put out weekly memos reporting what was happening in the school's fourteen classes in these areas, and held monthly meetings to discuss implementation. They also agreed to be available if teachers had particular concerns they would like to discuss individually. This has continued throughout the school year. Each classroom teacher has tended to pick one of the areas as the target for development during the year; a few teachers attend meetings, gather ideas, and experiment with ideas in all three areas. There is no pressure to be involved in changing instruction in any of the areas. However, because the teachers saw a need and asked for help, they are interested in making changes.

It seems likely that where professional growth is valued teachers will gain the knowledge they need to enable them to adapt their methods to the needs of students. Without a knowledge base, there is little foundation for encouraging innovation, experimentation, and adaptation.

Some problems and solutions

Keeping in mind and applying "All I can change is me" is not always easy for the staff. As fulfilling as the majority of the staff finds the challenge of meeting the needs of students with unique learning styles, everyone is not always open to change and those of us who guide change do not always present it in the most palatable and nonthreatening way. Let me share with you five of the problems we encountered and a few of the solutions that seemed to work.

Seeing no need to change

In the past it was not uncommon for me to detect a curriculum need, research it, attend conferences seeking answers to questions about it, and invite an expert to Benchmark to present the latest ideas on the subject, only to be disappointed a few months later when the staff had not made any real strides toward change. I learned slowly that the staff's discovery of the need for change must come before the ideas for change and that all this takes time. Seeing the need for change can be fostered by evaluating curriculum weaknesses, discussing professional literature related to the area of concern, exploring ideas with a supervisor, and setting up a pilot class for others to observe.

Equating the need for change with poor teaching

In Benchmark's early years, staff members interpreted suggestions for change, whether made to them individually or to the staff as a group, as evidence that the person making the suggestion was dissatisfied with their teaching. We have learned that we are much more successful in bringing about change if we use the less threatening approach of using a teacher's concern as an avenue to discussing possible changes or adaptations in practice. If a concern is not brought up by the teacher, we find we are more likely to have him/her discover a need for change if we model a new practice in the classroom or if we teach a teacher's class while she/he visits in another classroom. Modeling new practices and teaching a class for a teacher while she/he visits usually are not viewed as threatening to teachers if they are a common occurrence throughout the school and if one teacher has not been singled out for such attention. Often we suggest that two teachers share the preparation of a unit, as in social studies. This strategy tends to bring about change in teachers, and they enjoy both the camaraderie and the lighter work load.

Resisting change due to lack of time

Sometimes the staff asked for help in implementing a needed change, but I tended to introduce too many ideas. In such instances, the staff felt overwhelmed; they were sure they could never find time to prepare and implement the new ideas. Recently, we have tried to space the introduction of ideas or, when we present many ideas, to make it clear that we do not expect a teacher to implement every one. In addition, we have tried to give teachers support in dealing with time constraints. One way we have helped is to have administrators, supervisors, and coordinators prepare sample lessons for teachers. Another strategy is joint teacher planning. In August we hold voluntary preparation meetings where teachers work together on lesson planning and seatwork. Throughout the year, teachers are encouraged to continue working together and to borrow one another's plans, word cards, posters, or seatwork where appropriate. In the office, we maintain files of plans and worksheets for frequently used texts. Teachers rarely use these as originally designed, but looking at someone else's plan often speeds up preparation and gives teachers a sense of security in the way they are planning a lesson. Another tactic we use is to have supervisors teach while the teacher catches up on reports, preparations, and other paperwork. It is amazing how much more open to change teachers are when they feel on top of things.

Feeling that good teachers do not need to change

Teachers who have seemed to succeed in meeting the needs of all but a few of their students sometimes do not see a need to add more techniques to their repertoire. Often they are fearful of changing anything when what they have been doing usually works. Working with these old pros can take the most patience of all. Our most successful cases of change in the classrooms of experienced teachers have occurred when the teacher has elected to invite a special teacher into the room to take responsibility for piloting a new program for one period each day while the teacher acts as an assistant. This absolves teachers of responsibility and they are often more willing to go along with the innovation. A second strategy is to pair a teacher for team teaching with another teacher with whom she/he enjoys working and respects. When the resistant teacher sees students in the team member's classroom responding positively to the new technique, she/he is more likely to try it.

Confusing priorities about teacher creativity and students' needs

Some teachers feel they are giving up their right to be creative if they are expected to adopt an approach to teaching that is consistent, systematic, and sequential, even when such an approach is what the students need. These teachers need to feel that they have the freedom to do their own thing, to have a classroom characterized by diversity of routine, one that flows with what the students (or teacher) feel like doing on a particular day. Dealing with this issue requires care and tact in guiding the teacher to see what elements of the program need to be consistent, systematic, and sequential to best meet the needs of each child while still providing the teacher with the opportunity to implement creative ideas within the framework of the suggested program. We have found in such cases that change can be brought about if innovation is encouraged and rewarded when it is in keeping with the best interest of each student. For the most part, creativity for the sake of creativity is ignored. The teacher is often asked to share appropriate adaptations and innovations with other staff members. Teachers enjoy this recognition, and we find that the innovations tend to become more appropriate to meeting students' needs.

Summary

Helping teachers adapt to the needs of students with learning problems is an exciting challenge. When change results in higher staff morale and greater student progress, we find that being a change agent is as rewarding as it is challenging.

At Benchmark School, change to meet the needs of poor readers occurs in four major areas: Instructional practices, curriculum, policies, and priorities. These changes occur most readily when several factors exist. One factor is a satisfying and safe school climate. At Benchmark, this climate is characterized by a sense of excitement, high expectations, trust, and administrative responsiveness to staff needs. Second, we have discovered that the staff is more receptive to change when there is staff involvement in problem solving. The staff is involved in identifying problems, gathering data, discussing ideas, formulating solutions, and monitoring progress. Ownership of ideas is a third requisite for change. Ownership is developed by encouraging and supporting teachers as they try ideas and adapt them to the needs of their students. Fourth, we try to help teachers develop a knowledge base upon which they can base decisions for change.

Bringing about change is far from problem free. Some problems we have dealt with are teachers seeing no need to change, equating the need for change with poor teaching, resisting change due to lack of time, feeling that good teachers do not need to change, and confusing priorities about teacher creativity and students' needs. The keys to solving all of these problems involve understanding, attempting to solve the problem from the teacher's point of view, and individualizing supervisory techniques according to the developmental level of the teacher. Administrators and supervisors often have had to remind themselves that "All I can change is me" and "There is no best method" of helping teachers adapt to the needs of students with learning problems.

Reference

Gaskins, I.W., and Elliot, T.T. (Eds.). *Teaching for success: Administrative and classroom practices at Benchmark School.* Media, PA: Benchmark Press, 1983.

Prelude

H arry Singer and Thomas Bean have spent a great deal of time, collectively and individually, working with teachers to improve students' understanding of the kind of information laden texts they encounter in science and social science classrooms. In the process of their myriad and varied encounters, they have tried and evaluated various models of staff development. In this chapter they share with us their knowledge, experience, and expertise in these matters. Since they have worked so often and so closely with administrators, they have organized their ideas in the framework of a conversation, hypothetical but nonetheless illustrative, with a superintendent of a secondary school district. They present us with three models—an intern model intimately tied to a university setting; a more conventional inservice model; and an evolutionary model built on the assumption that if you are given no other options, then the best thing to do is to start working with one teacher on one issue. We think you will find their information useful and their approach stimulating.

Harry Singer
Thomas W. Bean

8

Three models for helping teachers to help students learn from text

We want you to listen in on a conversation we had recently with a school superintendent. The superintendent came to us and said, "I know you are both involved in teaching teachers how to help students learn from text at the secondary level. I'd like you to tell me how to do this in my district." Here's our reply and the dialogue that developed as we outlined various staff and student development models. We think the models being discussed may be useful to any superintendent or principal with a desire to orchestrate a staff development program in learning from text.

First, we want to give you some idea of what learning from text means and some of the problems confronting teachers and students. Then we will present our conversation in which we introduce three models of staff development—the intern model, the inservice model, and the evolutionary model.

Explanation of learning from text

When readers learn from text, they construct meaning as a result of an interaction between the reader's resources and a text's features (Singer, 1983; Tierney & Pearson, 1982). This definition assumes that only two parties are involved in the interaction: the student and the text.

However, in a classroom a third party affects this interaction in a variety of ways. The teacher can establish purposes and goals to be achieved in learning from text, instruct students in strategies for reaching these goals, devise tests that determine whether the goals have been reached, and feed this information back to the students (Singer, 1983; Singer & Bean 1982a, 1982b). The teacher also selects texts and can choose texts that are friendly (written in a way that facilitates comprehension, Singer, 1985) or unfriendly.

Even if a text is friendly, it is not likely to fit all students in a class because of the wide range of individual differences that exist in any class. We know when a heterogeneous group of students progresses through the grades, we can expect its range of reading achievement (in reading age equivalents) to increase from four years at grade one to twelve years at grade twelve. The general formula is that the range of reading age equivalents in a heterogeneous class is two-thirds of the median age of the group. This is also the average range in mental ability of a heterogeneous class. That is, if all students are achieving in reading up to their mental capability, this range in achievement will occur.

Fortunately, we have strategies for handling this wide range of individual differences in ability to learn from text. These strategies fall into two major categories: single and multiple text. Single text strategies assume that a teacher will adapt one text to meet the needs of all the students in the class. These strategies include marginal glosses, the SQ3R method, reading and learning from text guides, directed reading activities with active comprehension, and graphic organizers. Multiple text strategies assume that a teacher will use several texts on a given topic within one class. They include the inquiry, concept, and project (unit) methods (Singer & Donlan, 1980).

We can better explain learning from text in a classroom setting through the use of the instructional model shown in Figure 1. The model consists of four components: students, text (or lecture), test (or goal), and instructor. The model indicates that students interact with a text to achieve a goal, often in the form of a test. The instructor interacts with all three of the other components: an instructor can teach students how to learn from a friendly text or can modify the text to make it friendlier (for example, adding marginal glosses, devising reading guides, or inserting questions). The in-

Figure 1
Instructional model for learning from text in a classroom

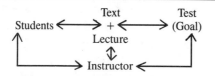

The model shows the interrelations among the model's major components. Coherence occurs when the instructor's objectives, the students' learning abilities, class purposes, materials (text or lecture) for satisfying those purposes, and the test for assessing those purposes are in agreement. The instructor influences the other three components and they, in turn, influence the instructor.

structor also defines the goals and constructs tests to determine whether students have attained these goals. One hypothesis we have been testing is that achievement in a classroom setting is likely to be highest when there is coherence among all the components depicted in our instructional model (Singer & Bean, 1982a, 1982b). In other words, to improve achievement you have to be concerned with all four components, not just one of them.

The conversation

With this background in place, we turn to our conversation with the superintendent.

Superintendent: "I can understand that learning from text is a complex activity, but what did you actually do in the districts where you developed programs?"

S & B: "We can best answer your question by describing each of our three programs and explaining how we operated them. Then we will answer any questions you have about doing similar projects in your district."

In each of these programs, we tried to merge all four components shown in Figure 1 into a coherent instructional program that would not only teach students how to learn from text but also achieve additional educational objectives.

Intern model

The purpose of our first program, an intern model for training content reading specialists, was to determine whether committed teachers who were trained to teach reading in the content areas at the junior high school level could improve the reading performance of all their students (Singer, 1973). Furthermore, we wanted our specialists to demonstrate that they could teach heterogeneous groups of students in regular content area classrooms using regular texts and without tracking, a practice associated with stigmatizing students to the point of decreasing their achievement. We anticipated that if the content reading specialists succeeded in teaching their own students to learn from text, the specialists would gain credibility with their colleagues and would be able to teach them to teach students to learn from text.

This program contrasts with those that expect students to learn how to read and learn from texts in developmental reading classes in elementary school or in special reading classes, reading laboratories, or pull out classes in junior high school and then to transfer and apply these skills on their own to all their content area classes. We assumed that teachers who were knowledgeable about the content of texts and who knew how to teach students to learn from text would be most qualified to teach students to learn content from text. Students would learn how to learn from texts in specific content areas and would not have to transfer their general skills to their content classes. We know from research that transfer of training does not have a high probability of occurrence. Therefore, it is best to teach something directly rather than rely on transfer from one situation to another.

As another contrast, instead of using full time consultants located in a central office, we used reading specialists who served in their schools as teachers for two-thirds of the day and were available as consultants for one-third of their time. They were knowledgeable about the school, staff, and students with whom they worked, so they were able to consult with full knowledge of the situation. In turn, teachers were able to see demonstrations in which the reading specialists taught the same students the teachers had in their own classes. Thus, our content reading specialists would combine expertise in their content areas with knowledge about learning from text. They would use this knowledge to teach their own students and then to disseminate their expertise to others on their faculties.

Specific objectives of the program

Our program had these specific objectives:

1. We wanted to improve the reading achievement of junior high students, particularly those who are educationally disadvantaged. Our intent was to attain statistical convergence in the achievement of Anglo and ethnic minority groups and, in general, to improve the average level of reading achievement in the junior high school.

2. We also wanted to prepare reading specialists for the junior high school. We taught our specialists to diagnose and remedy reading difficulties through course work and a year long supervised internship.

3. We planned to use our reading specialists to help all teachers in the junior high school to use successful approaches to teach content area reading. The teachers could then incorporate their knowledge into classroom practices in order to help all of their students.

4. We expected our content specialists to help improve the junior high school curriculum. Our program assumed that improved competence in the teachers' subject fields would increase their awareness of instructional options. Thus, the course work taken by our content reading specialists in a specific content area provided a knowledge base for enabling them to help improve the curriculum in their fields.

5. We expected each of the content reading specialists to develop a model classroom for the improvement of reading in a particular content area. We viewed development of these classrooms as a central objective of the project.

Installing the program in junior high schools

The first phase involved a year of university course work in which the teachers we recruited earned a master's degree with a joint speciality in reading and a content area. Thus, they learned to be reading content specialists. In the second phase, these reading content specialists began their intern year. We placed two interns in each of four junior high schools in two districts. Both school districts paid full salaries for the interns and provided them with one-third released time for consulting in their own schools. Principals in both school districts had volunteered their schools for this phase of the program and had participated in initial selection of candidates for the program.

General procedures

We used four approaches to teach content reading to heterogeneously grouped classes of seventh graders (and a few classes of eighth graders).

1. Our specialists taught units based on a project or theme method they had learned in a curriculum course during the first phase of the project. The units used a range of reading material encompassing all the reading ability levels in a classroom. (See Singer & Donlan, 1980, for an example of the project method.)
2. Specialists used reading and learning from text guides in each content area. These guides included word recognition and word meaning instruction; we had taught the content specialists how to construct these guides in one of their courses at the university, and they used this technique for their daily lesson plans. Figure 2 is an example of this type of guide.
3. Content reading specialists in English stressed group discussions, taught reading through writing activities, had students keep journals, used self-selected paperbacks during reading time, and used role playing and class plays (Moffett, 1968).
4. All the content reading specialists used cross ability teaching, sometimes in group settings and other times in one to one relationships.

The content reading specialists spent one-third of each day consulting with other teachers. They taught their colleagues how to

Singer, Bean

Figure 2
Reading and learning from text guide for a passage in a text

Text passage

Explanation of Earthquakes

The earth is made up of three layers. The surface is a
crust. The continents lie on the surface surrounded by water.
Next comes a layer called a mantle. Below it is a core of hot
liquid iron. The hot liquid rises up toward the surface like
bubbles in a pot simmering on a stove. As it does, it moves the
continents. This movement is the cause of earthquakes.

Reading and learning from text guide

Literal

Circle whether the statement is true (T) or false (F). Also indicate the line in the
text that tells you the answer.

			Line
1. The earth has three layers.	(T)	F	1
2. The *crust* is the name of the top layer.	(T)	F	1-2
3. The continents are on the surface.	(T)	F	2
4. Water is all around the continents.	(T)	F	2
5. The *mantle* is the name of the middle layer of the earth.	(T)	F	3
6. *Core* means the center of something.	(T)	F	3
7. The bottom layer is the mantle.	T	(F)	3
8. The center of the earth consists of hot liquid iron.	(T)	F	3-4

Interpretation

1. Hot liquid rises because it is lighter than cold liquid.	(T)	F	4
2. The continents cannot move because they are huge.	T	(F)	5
3. Earthquakes indicate a continent or part of it is moving.	(T)	F	6

Generalization

In small discussion groups decide whether the following statements are generally
true and apply to this passage.

1. Change is the law of life.	Applies	Does not apply
2. Movement is always going on in the earth.	Applies	Does not apply

use study guides and how to work with small groups. They also demonstrated reading strategies to a class and the teacher, then had the teacher use the same strategy on the next lesson. To encourage teachers to consult and to provide the means for curriculum modification, we gave each junior high school $2,500 for purchase of materials and supplies. Purchase decisions were to grow out of consultation between teachers and the reading content specialists.

Data

To determine whether our project had improved students' achievement, we gathered data in the content reading specialists' classes and in control group classes of comparable students. The control group classes were taught by teachers who volunteered to have their classes tested in the fall and retested in May. It was not feasible to randomly assign students to experimental and control group treatments.

We used three test batteries for gathering data: California Reading Achievement Test, Junior High School Level, Forms w and x; Carter's California Study Methods Test (CTB/McGraw-Hill); and Athey and Holmes' Reading Personality Scale (1969).

Results

The standardized test results were statistically insignificant, indicating that no generalized improvement had occurred as compared with a control group. However, the project did demonstrate that it was possible for content reading specialists to teach a class of junior high school pupils without tracking students or subdividing them into groups of high, average, and low reading achievers. In a school district consisting of about 6 percent Black, 12 percent Chicano, and 82 percent Anglo students, our heterogeneously grouped classes showed no relative loss in reading achievement when compared with more homogeneously grouped classes.

If we were making the comparison today, as we have done in our more recent studies (Singer & Donlan, 1982), we would use criterion referenced tests. Because these tests are sensitive to instructional effects, we would know whether our strategies make a difference in student achievement. We do know that low achieving students often remarked that they answered more questions correctly on their reading and learning from text guides than they ever did before in answering questions on their texts.

Evaluation

Our intern program was effective. The reading content specialists successfully achieved one of their purposes: to establish demonstration classrooms. The consultant role of the content reading specialists was also successful, but only after two-thirds of a school year had gone by. We found it took that long for the content reading specialists to develop demonstration classrooms, gain credibility as specialists, and develop rapport with their faculties. Their dissemination procedures were diverse: helping with problem readers, working with small groups in a teacher's class, and conversing informally with other teachers in the faculty lounge. Gradually they began to teach the teachers how to teach the entire class to learn from text.

Institutionalization of the project

The project also had a significant impact on our program in training reading content specialists at the University of California in Riverside. Because of the project, we learned what we had to do at the university to develop content reading specialists for the schools. We also learned a great deal about teaching students how to learn from texts. We now have all reading specialist candidates go through a two stage sequence of courses. The first stage is a four course concentration for reading and writing instruction taken during the preservice program. The second stage consists of a master's degree divided into four groups of courses: (1) reading theory, diagnosis, improvement of reading and learning from text, and learning theory; (2) curriculum and instructional strategies and children's and adolescents' literature; (3) evaluation and critical reading of research; and (4) an internship involving a seminar and supervising beginning reading teachers.

Some forty-five content reading specialists have completed the program and now are serving as reading specialists in elementary, junior high, and senior high schools throughout southern California. Ideally, we would like the content reading specialists in junior or senior high schools to teach their own classes for at least one period a day, direct content reading acquisition classes or laboratories for one or two periods, diagnose students and advise them and their parents for one period, and consult or provide inservice training with faculty members one period.

S & B: "That explains our intern model. Do you have any questions?"

Superintendent: "Well, your program took two years and had external funding and university support. How can I take over that sort of program?"

S & B: "Some of the procedures are provided in our description of the program. For example, you would need to select teachers in your area to return to the local university for a master's degree in reading with a content area emphasis in a secondary school subject. They would need a sabbatical with pay for the first year. During the second year they would need a teaching assignment that provided two-thirds regular content teaching and one-third released time."

Superintendent: "Why would they need released time?"

S & B: "So they can work with other teachers and diagnose problems, consult with parents, and do demonstration teaching in their own and other classrooms. When other teachers become confident in the content specialists' help, you spread the benefit of your first year investment to all teachers in the school."

Superintendent: "Wouldn't it be better if they were released full time?"

S & B: "They need opportunities in their own classes to apply what they have learned. Moreover, having their own content class increases their credibility with other teachers who have students like their own."

Superintendent: "How many content reading specialists should I have per school?"

S & B: "We had two per junior high school so they could reinforce one another's efforts and cover more than one content area."

Superintendent: "In my district that would mean twelve teachers."

S & B: "Ideally, you want all students to develop further their ability to learn from text. To cover all students in a school, each reading specialist should be able to (1) teach a demonstration content class for at least one period; (2) help students who are still learning how to read for one to two periods; (3) have one period per day to work with other teachers in a phase in, phase out strategy; and (4) have one period for preparation and parent consultation. Given this course load for a content reading specialist, we think you would want one content reading specialist per 1,000 students."

Superintendent: "What is a 'phase in, phase out' strategy?"

S & B: "An ideal way to teach another teacher a learning from text strategy is first to demonstrate the strategy with a lesson for the teacher's own class. Then, have the teacher prepare another lesson using the same strategy with the reading specialist's help. Finally, have the teacher use the strategy independently. This is the phase out portion."

Superintendent: "If the district can't afford this program, what are the alternatives?"

S & B: "If a foundation, private firm, or government grant isn't available, you might be able to recruit some already trained content area specialists. Or there are some other staff development models we have tried that work quite well. We'll describe our inservice model for you."

Inservice model

Perhaps because of reduced teacher mobility and reduced hiring of new teachers to solve staffing needs, we have observed that intensive, long range inservice programs on learning from text are replacing brief, one shot efforts. This is certainly the case in the Anaheim Union High School District in California. The district has conducted a large, districtwide inservice project involving a group of thirty well informed content area teachers, reading specialists, and administrators. These project members collaborate in the planning and implementation of school and department level inservice for their colleagues, potentially influencing hundreds of additional teachers and students. We will give you the history of the Anaheim inservice model, a model that could be adapted in similar urban districts.

Purpose

Initial planning for a districtwide effort in learning from text began in Spring 1982. The impetus for the effort grew out of falling test scores. A series of planning sessions involving the assistant superintendent, curriculum director, reading specialists, content representatives, and a university reading professor resulted in the four year model.

We wanted to provide content area teachers at the junior and senior high levels with an array of learning from text strategies (Readence, Bean, & Baldwin, 1981; Singer & Donlan, 1980). These strategies, in the broad areas of vocabulary and comprehension, are designed to teach students to read and respond to challenging content area assignments.

One of the assumptions that guided us in the planning stages was the need for teachers to experience directly learning from text strategies. This assumption suggested that a small group approach would be most appropriate.

District funding provided support for two week, half day summer workshop sessions. Participating teachers were paid a stipend and, during the next year, they were to have some released time to work with colleagues and orchestrate workshops for faculty. During the summer of 1982, a group of fifteen junior high content teachers met with Thomas Bean and three district reading specialists. These teachers represented six schools and more than twelve content areas.

Our overall objective in the workshop was to develop a resource handbook of sample lessons exemplifying vocabulary and comprehension strategies. This handbook would be used during the regular academic year in staff development sessions. The first week of the workshop focused on prereading and postreading strategies in the area of technical vocabulary. Participants considered strategies such as graphic organizers and categorization. During the second week, comprehension strategies were considered, including anticipation/reaction guides and selective reading and study guides.

The workshop format followed our assumption that teachers need to experience and experiment with a new strategy. Four steps were integral to this process of assimilating a new strategy.

Figure 3
Graphic organizer on running

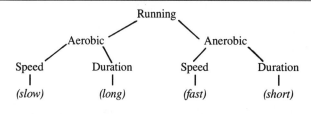

1. Each instructional strategy was introduced through a simulation lesson and walk through of the strategy purpose and steps. For example, we introduced the strategy of a graphic organizer for a general topic — running. The graphic organizer for this topic is shown in Figure 3. We instructed the participants to read to identify the speed and duration differences in these two contrasting forms of running. Then they had to insert the information into the blank spaces in the postreading organizer (as shown in the parentheses). After this strategy, we had the teachers find various patterns of organization in text and construct a graphic organization for their own textbook and teaching materials.

2. Following the simulation, we had the workshop participants meet in small groups clustered by content areas. They used a handout summarizing strategy steps to create an example lesson in their own content material.

3. Workshop participants then gave their lesson a trial run by teaching it to a colleague from a different content area.

4. Edited example lesson plans then became part of the handbook. The sample lesson in Figure 4 illustrates this step (Rayl, 1983). We distributed the handbooks to faculty throughout the district during the first week of class. The handbooks are used in school and department level staff development sessions with assistance from the members of our project team.

Figure 4
Example lesson plan

Name of strategy
  Anticipation guide

Subject area
  Physical education (stretching)

Source
  (Text and chapter pages)

  Hayes, Ash. *Fit to Be You.* Series of three films, twelve minutes each. San Diego, CA: Walt Disney Educational Media, 1981.

Purpose

  To challenge or support students' current beliefs about a content topic. Group the statements into three levels: (1) textually explicit (literal or factual), (2) textually implicit (interpretation or inferencing), (3) experiential (application or problem solving).

Steps

  1. Identify the major concepts and supporting details in text handouts, lectures, and films.
  2. Identify students' experiences and beliefs that will be challenged.
  3. Create statements that reflect your students' prediscussion notions or beliefs.

  Examples:

Before Yes/No	After Yes/No	*Level 1*
_____	_____	1. When stretching, it is helpful to use bouncing movements.
_____	_____	2. Muscles used during vigorous activity should be stretched after the activity.
_____	_____	3. Tightening the antagonistic muscle group will help relax the muscles being stretched.
_____	_____	4. Five to ten seconds is enough time to achieve flexibility in a joint.

  Level 2

_____	_____	1. Stretching is not necessary in hot weather.
_____	_____	2. If you want to stay loose, don't lift weights.
_____	_____	3. Tight ligaments, tendons, and muscles are less susceptible to strain or tearing.
_____	_____	4. The only value to stretching is reduction of injuries.

Singer, Bean

Figure 4
Example lesson plan (continued)

Level 3

_____	_____	1. Most doctors prescribe stretching for relief of tension and stress.
_____	_____	2. A gymnast and a football player should stretch about the same length of time.
_____	_____	3. Stretching is neglected because it is painful and boring.
_____	_____	4. Stretching with the aid of a partner can bring about greater flexibility.

Take home term
Proprioceptive neuromuscular facilitation

Evaluating the project

Early in the planning stages we decided to use a long range evaluation process with the following three components: (1) summer workshop evaluation of individual strategies introduced, (2) department and school evaluation of dissemination workshop strategies, and (3) classroom level observation and interviews with teachers and students. At this stage of the project we can comment on the first evaluation component, which has served as a guide in devising department and school level workshops.

First and second year summer workshops

During the first summer, ten junior high content teachers explored twelve vocabulary and comprehension strategies. At the close of each of the week long sessions, they rated each strategy using a five point semantic differential gauging how applicable they felt a particular strategy might be in their content area. For example:

Graphic organizers are
applicable _____ not applicable _____

In planning department and school staff development for the coming year, we focused on the top three ranked strategies our summer participants selected. The vocabulary strategies were preview in context, graphic organizers, and list-group-label.

Preview in context is a prereading introduction using four to six important vocabulary words (Readence, Bean, & Baldwin, 1981). Students use the surrounding sentence context to predict possible definitions. Since technical vocabulary is an integral part of all content areas, this strategy was particularly applicable for our participants. Similarly, graphic organizers are useful for guiding pre and postreading stages. Moreover, they can be applied by students as an independent study strategy (Bean et al., 1986). List-group-label is a logical postreading extension of the first two strategies since it involves categorization of technical terms (Bean, Ryan, & Inabinette, 1983).

The three comprehension strategies viewed most positively by our junior high group were anticipation reaction guides, directed listening lessons, and study guide questions.

Anticipation reaction guides are relatively easy to develop. They consist of statements that challenge students' thinking about text, film, or lecture concepts (Readence, Bean, & Baldwin, 1981). Hence, they are readily adaptable to a variety of instructional contexts. Directed listening lessons and study guides, while taking more teacher time to develop, provide good pre and postreading guidance.

During the second summer, tenth and eleventh grade teachers from various content areas also explored and evaluated a number of vocabulary and comprehension strategies. Their top three vocabulary strategies were graphic organizers, list-group-label, and preview in context. Their top three comprehension strategies were anticipation reaction guides, selective reading guides, and study guide questions.

These summer evaluations have been extremely helpful in devising workshop sessions for department and school faculty. Workshop sessions during the school year rarely span more than a single day. Based on the summer evaluations, we have been introducing teachers to broadly based strategies such as graphic organizers and guide material. Although we have seen many of these strategies become a part of the content teachers' repertoire, we have not yet collected systematic observation and interview data. However, we can perceive that learning from text is becoming part of the culture of the Anaheim district teachers. This cultural diffusion model, which took at least three or four years to reach this stage, is a major improvement on the one shot inservice model attempted by many districts in the past. You can see why a long term approach is necessary.

Superintendent: "Yes, I can see how a district with a well established faculty might benefit from the approach you just described. I am curious about how much this program would cost a district. Can you give me an approximate cost breakdown?"

S & B: "Naturally, the major cost factor involves personnel. For a summer half day, two week workshop, the cost might be $2,000 for a consultant, $8,000 for teacher stipends, and $1,000 for materials — a total of $11,000. For each followup session during the academic year, the cost might be $400 for a consultant and $800 for substitutes to provide released time for twenty teachers, a total of $1,200. Thus, we would estimate the total cost for a year long program to be somewhere between $20,000 and $25,000."

Superintendent: "That doesn't seem unreasonable given the obvious benefits to teachers and students. But what can I do if no funds are available in a particular year and I want to initiate a small scale effort to improve students' learning from text?"

S & B: "Well, there are other, smaller scale approaches to staff development that can evolve into a larger effort as funding becomes available. We initiated such an evolutionary project at the individual classroom level. This project involved a single teacher in the planning, development, and applied research stages of learning from text (see Wade, 1983). We'll describe our small scale project and suggest some ways you might go about initiating something similar in your district."

Evolutionary model

In order to evaluate selected learning from text strategies in a systematic fashion, we devised a three year applied research project. Then we set out to find a teacher to collaborate with us. We wanted to work with a teacher and school that had not been inundated with a vast amount of staff development in learning from text. We found

Figure 5
Construction of a graphic organizer

1. *Selection:* Write the topic sentence.

   "What reasons motivated European countries to explore and expand their horizons?"

2. *Diagram:*

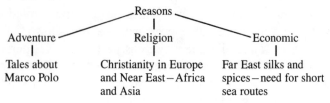

3. *Generalization:* Three major reasons motivated Europe to expand its horizons, but the most important was economic trade.

Jack Sorter, a history teacher at Garden Grove High School.

In a series of planning meetings with Sorter, we read and discussed much of the available work on summarization and graphic organizer strategies. Based on these discussions, we designed a series of applied instructional experiments in Sorter's classroom. In the most recent experiment, we were able to show that students taught how to construct their own graphic organizers of world history concepts, such as the one in Figure 5, significantly outperformed a comparable class that used a traditional outlining approach (Bean et al., 1986). In addition, we found that students in the graphic organizer group were better able to reconstruct ideas from poorly structured text in order to write a succinct, well formed summary.

These data based findings are important, as are the ideas about staff development that emerged as we collaborated with Sorter. For example, we began with a procedure for constructing graphic organizers that Sorter modified to better reflect the specific structure of world history text. He instructed students to place background information from their reading on the left side of the graphic

Figure 6
Graphic organizer on the industrial revolution in Japan

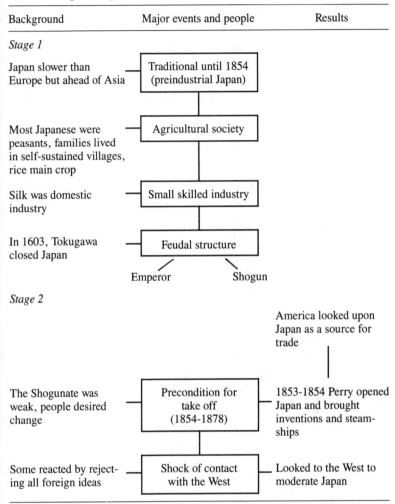

Background	Major events and people	Results

Stage 1

Japan slower than Europe but ahead of Asia — Traditional until 1854 (preindustrial Japan)

Most Japanese were peasants, families lived in self-sustained villages, rice main crop — Agricultural society

Silk was domestic industry — Small skilled industry

In 1603, Tokugawa closed Japan — Feudal structure

Emperor   Shogun

Stage 2

America looked upon Japan as a source for trade

The Shogunate was weak, people desired change — Precondition for take off (1854-1878) — 1853-1854 Perry opened Japan and brought inventions and steamships

Some reacted by rejecting all foreign ideas — Shock of contact with the West — Looked to the West to moderate Japan

organizer, major events in the middle, and results of these events on the right, as shown in Figure 6. This concrete structure helped students use graphic organizers in a fashion that would not have been readily apparent to a reading professor. More recently, Sorter has begun using students' graphic organizers as a basis for teaching them how to make predictions about upcoming events in world history text. He is effectively overcoming one of the major pitfalls of most content area texts: cursory coverage of a topic that will not be explained or mentioned again in future chapters, a consequence of the way high school history texts have been written for the past thirty years (Fitzgerald, 1979).

We have learned a great deal through working closely with Jack Sorter, but the most interesting aspect of this evolutionary approach is the influence Sorter has had on his colleagues at Garden Grove High School and within the district. This influence has not come about through any administrator's suggestion that teachers should pay attention to Sorter's class and to his learning from text approach. Instead, his students have been the ambassadors.

Toward the end of the first year of our project, two of Sorter's students who were also taking a biology class found that graphic organizers were helpful in studying difficult sections of the biology text. They showed their graphic organizers for their biology text to their teacher. He became interested in learning more about graphic organizers. The next year, the biology teacher helped us conduct an applied instructional experiment in three of his biology classes.

Superintendent: "I can see how this last, small scale model contains features of the two larger scale staff development efforts. But where would I find someone with a desire to work individually with teachers in my district?"

S & B: "Most university schools of education have content reading professors and graduate students who are interested in collaborating with content teachers on applied research. *Reading in the Content Areas: Research for Teachers* (Dupuis, 1984) provides a fairly comprehensive listing of content reading professors who have authored textbooks in this area. The list appears at the end of this chapter. It should be helpful in tracking the expert help you are looking for."

Superintendent: "This discussion has been very helpful. Now I have three models I can use in my discussions with principals, curriculum coordinators, and my board. We will decide which model fits our situation and budget and then we can get moving on the planning stages of a learning from text project."

References

Athey, I., and Holmes, J.A. *Reading success and personality characteristics in junior high school students.* University of California Publication in Education, 18. Berkeley, CA: University of California Press, 1969.

Bean, T.W., Ryan, R., and Inabinette, N. The effect of a list-group-label strategy on the acquisition of technical vocabulary. *Reading Psychology,* 1983, *4,* 247-252.

Bean, T.W., Singer, H., Sorter, J., and Frazee, C. The effect of metacognitive instruction in outlining and graphic organizer construction on students' comprehension in a tenth grade world history class. *Journal of Reading Behavior,* 1986, *18,* 153-169.

Dupuis, M.M. *Reading in the content areas: Research for teachers.* Newark, DE: International Reading Association, 1984.

Fitzgerald, F. *America revisited: History schoolbooks in the twentieth century.* Boston: Little, Brown, 1979.

Moffett, J. *A student centered language arts curriculum, grades K-13: A handbook for teachers.* New York: Houghton Mifflin, 1968.

Rayl, D. Anticipation guide for stretching in physical education. *Reading and learning from text course of study.* Anaheim, CA: Anaheim Union High School District, 1983, 67-68.

Readence, J.E., Bean, T.W., and Baldwin, R.S. *Content area reading: An integrated approach.* Dubuque, IA: Kendall/Hunt, 1981.

Singer, H. Criteria for selecting friendly texts. In E.K. Dishner, T.W. Bean, J.E. Readence, and D.W. Moore (Eds.), *Content area reading: Improving classroom instruction.* Dubuque, IA: Kendall/Hunt, 1985.

Singer, H. History of the substrata factor theory of reading and its conceptual relationship to interaction theory. In L. Gentile, M. Kamil, and J. Blanchard (Eds.), *Content area reading: Improving classroom instruction.* Dubuque, IA: Kendall/Hunt, 1985.

Singer, H. *Preparation of reading content specialists for the junior high school.* 1973. (ED 088 003)

Singer, H., and Bean, T. (Eds.). *Learning from text project: Conceptualization, prediction, and intervention.* 1982b. (ED 223 989)

Singer, H., and Bean, T. (Eds.) *Proceedings of the Lake Arrowhead conference on learning from text, April 1982.* 1982a. (ED 222 860)

Singer, H., and Donlan, D. Active comprehension: Problem solving schema with question generation for comprehension of complex short stories. *Reading Research Quarterly,* 1982, *17*(2), 166-186.

Singer, H., and Bean, T. (Eds.). *Reading and learning from text.* Boston: Little, Brown, 1980.

Tierney, R.J., and Pearson, P.D. Learning to learn from text: A framework for improving classroom practice. In L. Reed and S. Ward (Eds.), *Basic skills: Issues and choices.* St. Louis, MO: CEMREL, 1982.

Wade, S. A synthesis of the research for improving reading in the social studies. *Review of Educational Research,* 1983, *53,* 461-497.

Texts in the field of content area reading*

Allington, R., and Strange, M. *Learning through reading in the content areas.* Lexington, MA: D.C. Heath, 1980.

Askov, E.N., and Kamm, K. *Study skills in the content areas.* Boston: Allyn & Bacon, 1982.

Aukerman, R.C. *Reading in the secondary school classroom.* New York: McGraw-Hill, 1972.

Aulls, M.W. *Developmental and remedial reading in the middle grades.* Boston: Allyn & Bacon, 1978.

Brunner, J.F., and Campbell, J.J. *Participating in secondary reading: A practical approach.* Englewood Cliffs, NJ: Prentice-Hall, 1978.

*Reprinted from M.M. Dupuis, *Reading in the content areas: Research for teachers.* Newark, DE: International Reading Association, 1984.

Burmeister, L.E. *Reading strategies for secondary school teachers,* second edition. Reading, MA: 1978.

Buron, A., and Claybaugh, A.L. *Using reading to teach subject matter: Fundamentals for content teachers.* Columbus, OH: Charles E. Merrill, 1974.

Cunningham, J.W., Cunningham, P.M., and Arthur, S.V. *Middle and secondary school reading.* New York: Longman, 1981.

Dillner, M.H., and Olson, J.P. *Personalizing reading instruction in middle, junior, and senior high schools, utilizing a competency based instructional system.* New York: Macmillan, 1977.

Dishner, E.K., Bean, T.W., and Readence, J.E. *Reading in the content areas: Improving classroom instruction.* Dubuque, IA: Kendall/Hunt, 1981.

Estes, T.H., and Vaughan, J.L., Jr. *Reading and learning in the content classroom.: Diagnostic and instructional strategies.* Boston: Allyn & Bacon, 1978.

Forgan, H.W., and Mangrum, C.T. *Teaching content area reading skills: A modular preservice and inservice program,* second edition. Columbus, OH: Charles E. Merrill, 1981.

Hafner, L.E. *Developmental reading in middle and secondary schools: Foundations, strategies, and skills for teaching.* New York: Macmillan, 1977.

Hafner, L.E. *Improving reading in middle and secondary schools: Selected readings,* second edition. New York: Macmillan, 1974.

Herber, H.L. *Teaching reading in content areas,* second edition. Englewood Cliffs, NJ: Prentice-Hall, 1978.

Hill, W.R. *Secondary school reading: Process, program, procedure.* Boston: Allyn & Bacon, 1979.

Karlin, R. *Teaching reading in high school,* second edition. Indianapolis, IN: Bobbs-Merrill, 1972.

Lamberg, W., and Lamb, C.E. *Reading instruction in the content areas.* Chicago: Rand-McNally, 1980.

Manning, M.M., and Manning, G.L. *Reading instruction in the middle school.* Washington, DC: National Education Association, 1979.

Miller, W.H. *Teaching reading in the secondary school.* Springfield, IL: Charles C Thomas, 1974.

Olson, A., and Ames, W. *Teaching reading skills in the secondary schools.* Scranton, PA: Intext Educational, 1972.

Readence, J.E., Bean, T.W., and Baldwin, R.S. *Content area reading: An integrated approach.* Dubuque, IA: Kendall/Hunt, 1981.

Robinson, H.A. *Teaching reading and study strategies: The content areas,* second edition. Boston: Allyn & Bacon, 1978.

Roe, B.D., Stoodt, B.D., and Burns, P.C. *Reading instruction in the secondary schools,* revised edition. Chicago: Rand-McNally, 1978.

Shepherd, D.L. *Comprehensive high school reading methods,* third edition. Columbus, OH: Charles E. Merrill, 1982.

Singer, H., and Donlan, D. *Reading and learning from text.* Boston: Little, Brown, 1980.

Smith, C.B., and Elliott, P.G. *Reading activities for middle and secondary schools: A handbook for teachers.* New York: Holt, Rinehart and Winston, 1979.

Smith, C.B., Smith, S.L., and Mikulecky, L. *Teaching reading in secondary school content subjects: A bookthinking process.* New York: Holt, Rinehart and Winston, 1978.

Smith, R.J., and Barrett, T.C. *Teaching reading in the middle grades,* second edition. Reading, MA: Addison-Wesley, 1979.

Thomas, E.L., and Robinson, H.A. *Improving reading in every class: A sourcebook for teachers,* second edition. Boston: Allyn & Bacon, 1982.

Tonjes, M.J., and Zintz, M.V. *Teaching reading/thinking/study skills in content classrooms.* Dubuque, IA: William C. Brown, 1981.

Vacca, R.T. *Content area reading.* Boston: Little, Brown, 1981.

Prelude

If you were to ask 1,000 randomly selected secondary reading teachers where the "mecca" of secondary reading was, you might expect to hear the names of large cities, especially those with universities nearby. But you would be wrong; those who are in the know will tell you that some of the most exciting things in secondary reading are happening in Kalispell, Montana. Things are happening there because Carol Santa has established a model of teacher change that is the rival of any in the world. Santa uses the notion of teacher as researcher to help her secondary content teachers learn that they possess more professional prerogative than they ever believed possible. Santa accomplishes this with a few very simple, down to earth concepts. Administratively, there appears to be a strong directed development tone to this project; yet the spirit of the research efforts themselves is very much in the mutual adaptation tradition.

9

Carol M. Santa

Changing teacher behavior in content reading through collaborative research

I n this chapter I describe the development of a content reading and writing project that produced a fundamental instructional change in our school system. We decided that our high school students simply were not learning as much as they should in our curriculum. We wanted to improve students' learning in all of their courses and make them better able to learn during their formal education and beyond.

With this goal of improved learning in mind, we began our change process. We first examined our present curriculum to determine the status of content reading instruction and came up with some general instructional goals. Next, we developed a theoretical framework for the project and began identifying instructional strategies that reflected this theoretical rationale. The key to the next stage, the implementation and evaluation of instructional strategies, was involving teachers in collaborative research. This involvement turned out to be a very powerful and sensitive approach for promoting fundamental changes in teaching. We then documented successful strategies in instructional manuals teachers used to disseminate the project to their colleagues.

With this overview in mind, I will now describe in more detail the various stages in the development of our successful content reading program.

Evaluation of present curriculum

We examined our curriculum and noted that education in our system was divided in purpose. The early grades focused on fundamental skills of reading, learning, and communication; by the middle of elementary school, the emphasis shifted to teaching specific content rather than fundamental learning skills; and in junior and senior high school, the transition was virtually complete. Teachers perceived themselves as content specialists and assumed that students had acquired the requisite reading and learning skills needed to master content material. We began to question this basic assumption. Perhaps our curriculum should not be so strongly divided between teaching reading and learning skills versus teaching content material. Perhaps content mastery could be enhanced if we tried to continue reading and learning skills within the context of specific course material. This type of change is difficult because it crosses the entire curriculum and requires a modification in attitude and approach for nearly all teachers and students.

Theoretical framework

Our teachers were able to begin making this shift from focusing strictly on content after they understood a few theoretical notions about reading and learning. In fact, three theoretical premises from cognitive psychology provided us with a framework for change, and all three were eventually reflected in all instructional components. First, we examined the role of organization in both learning and text structure. Second, we learned that instruction should be designed to involve the student as an active learner capable of integrating information with existing knowledge. Third, we wanted to emphasize the use of a variety of organizational strategies and the use of metacognitive or self-monitoring procedures.

Textbook organization

Although textbooks are the cornerstone of secondary education, our content teachers did not understand how the writing style and presentation of information in textbooks influence comprehensibility. Their choice of texts was based either on content covered or on standard readability formulas.

Few teachers quibble with the notion that texts should promote learning and help students understand important information. We wanted our teachers to understand that structure or coherence of text can dramatically affect its utility as a learning tool. We began with an introduction to basic research on the structure of text and its influence on comprehension.

I presented teachers with some of this research, and they examined whether their own texts contained characteristics of what Armbruster and Anderson (1981) have called "considerate text." They learned to evaluate text according to how clearly its authors organized the information. This included examining the overall structure of text — the presence of glossaries, study questions, and an organized and sensible table of contents. Their assessment also included careful examination of chapter and paragraph organization. They evaluated whether chapters contained preview or introductory paragraphs and summary statements. They also examined boldface titles and subtitles to determine if they reflected the important information developed in the text. They looked for explicit statements of importance, such as "the most important point is...." Other areas noted were the presence or absence of main ideas in paragraphs; the consistency of main idea placement; and specific paragraph structure such as problem solution, simple listing, comparison and contrast, and temporal sequencing.

Teachers found the most difficulty with texts at the paragraph or multiparagraph level. The most common problem was that main ideas typically were presented implicitly rather than explicitly. Teachers became aware that such inferential organization was lost on the poorer reader. Teachers also noted that their texts often contained extraneous information and excessive details that distracted students from learning important information. These insights helped teachers to understand some of the problems facing their students who were trying to use text to learn new information.

The teachers also began focusing on how text authors developed new vocabulary through context. They itemized the prevalent types of contextual information provided: direct definitions, restatements, comparisons, inferences, and examples. In the ideal situation, new vocabulary should be presented directly and then followed by elucidating examples and discussion. In many instances, teachers found authors had supplied few if any contextual aids. This understanding helped set the stage for the development of specific strategies for teaching students how to use the available context for learning new vocabulary.

Finally, teachers evaluated the presentation of visual information – charts, graphs, pictures. Are visual presentations relevant to the written text? Have authors provided verbal cues within text to focus the reader's attention on specific information? Is visual information located appropriately, within one or two pages of the written material, or does the reader have to flip back and forth on a visual hunt? If this is the case, visual information is simply too inconvenient to use.

Many teachers were surprised to learn just how inconsiderate their texts were. They began to understand one reason why they had been accomplishing immediate curriculum objectives by telling students the content of their reading assignments. Understanding the potential effect of text structure helped our teachers see the need for teaching students to read both considerate and inconsiderate text. Our teachers started making better, more sophisticated decisions regarding text adoptions. Even more important, the teachers began developing instructional strategies for helping students use text structure to improve their comprehension.

Background knowledge and active learning

The typical instructional format in content classes is for the teacher to assign students to read with little or no preparation. Our teachers needed to understand research regarding the link between background knowledge and reading comprehension. Rather than lecturing teachers about research on schemata or the influence of background knowledge on comprehension, I found it effective to make my point through a demonstration.

A selection that served this purpose well came from a study by Dooling and Lachman (1971) published in the *Journal of Experimental Psychology*. I instructed the teachers to listen to the following selection and then recall what they had heard:

> With hocked gems financing him our hero bravely defied all scornful laughter that tried to prevent his scheme. "Your eyes deceived," he had said. "An egg not a table correctly typifies this unexplored planet." Now three sturdy sisters sought proof. Forging along sometimes through calm vastness. Yet more often over turbulent peaks and valleys. Days became weeks as many doubters spread fearful rumors about the edge. At last from somewhere, welcomed winged creatures appeared signifying momentous success.

Naturally, the teachers had difficulty remembering anything from the selection. However, before the second trial we discussed what we knew about Columbus discovering America. Dramatic improvement in retention occurred after the second trial.

This demonstration made content teachers acutely aware that integrating new information with prior knowledge is truly the heart of comprehension. We presented research reinforcing the idea that a reader's prior knowledge is an exceptionally important determiner of comprehension (Baker & Stein, 1981; Schallert, 1982). Then teachers were ready to consider implications for teaching. They considered several questions: How can I find out what students know about a topic? How can I use this knowledge to guide my students' comprehension? What knowledge should be developed before my students read? Teachers began to understand that a major goal was to change instructional emphasis from postreading to prereading activities involving the development of relevant concepts and vocabulary.

The next theoretical area our teachers needed to understand was the effect of active, student generated strategies on learning content information. Again, I found that a demonstration coupled with a brief discussion of research provided the foundation for change. I began by engaging the teacher participants in a reading and studying paradigm modeled after a series of classic experiments conducted by Gates (1917). Half of the teachers read and reread a selection while the others followed a read/recall, read/recall sequence. Then both groups wrote down everything they could from the selection. Teachers in the more active read/recall condition remembered more.

The demonstration naturally evolved into a productive discussion about helping students focus attention on the reading task. That discussion inspired development of learning and reading strategies requiring greater cognitive effort than typically occurs in a secondary classroom. A description of several other experiments documented the effectiveness of student generated questions (Andre & Anderson, 1979), written and oral summaries (Ross, 1976; Stotsky, 1983) and notetaking (Santa, Abrahms, & Santa, 1979). The teachers learned that any of these strategies are effective as long as they help students focus their attention on the learning task and are appropriate for the type of test or criterion task (Anderson & Armbruster, 1982).

In addition to helping students become more actively engaged in their own learning, teachers need to help students become more aware of their own comprehension and studying. At this point I introduced teachers to recent research on metacognition or comprehension monitoring.

Metacognition

Metacognition is the idea that good readers are aware of their own cognitive activities while reading and know how to use and control their strategies to read, learn, and remember information. Rather than beginning with a formal discussion of research on metacognition, I began by describing an informal study conducted in several of our own junior level biology and history classes. After presenting biology students with a scientific article to read, I asked them to write a paragraph about how they would read and study the selection for a test. While many of the better students did use a variety of specific strategies, the average to low students had very poorly defined ideas about how to learn new information from reading. I recommended that teachers conduct a similar informal investigation with their own students.

We then discussed why the results were so predictable in light of current research on metacognition. As noted by Baker (1980) and Brown (1983), immature readers do not know if they have succeeded in comprehending and are unaware of strategies for obtaining meaning from text. Mature readers, on the other hand, are more strategic; they monitor how well they are comprehending and know when and how to call forth a variety of procedures to fix up their comprehension when necessary. The teachers also learned that such maturity does not necessarily evolve naturally. Rather, students need specific guidance so they can become more aware of the effect specific strategies have on their comprehension.

We then brainstormed ways to help students become more metacognitive. The teachers decided that they should help their students become competent in a variety of reading and studying strategies. They wanted their students to be able to choose which of several strategies would be most effective for a particular learning situation. In addition, they saw the need for more class discussion focusing on students' awareness of their own performance. For example, when students performed well on an examination, teachers began having those students describe strategies that led to their success. The means became as important as the end.

Thus, teachers began to change their instructional philosophies after understanding a few theoretical constructs. These constructs also served to focus teachers' ideas about particular learning strategies. For example, does a particular strategy help students link what they know to what they are about to learn? Is the strategy active and does it help students learn to monitor their own reading performance? Given a positive response to these questions, teachers felt confident that their innovations were worthy of classroom validation.

Teachers as collaborative researchers

Armed with this simple theoretical structure, teachers proceeded to the more difficult task of developing specific instructional applications and evaluating their ideas experimentally in real classroom situations. Involving teachers as researchers turned out to be a very sensitive and successful way to change teaching behavior. Research collaboration not only preserved teacher ownership of the project but provided convincing evidence to motivate change. Moreover, classroom based research provided a systematic procedure for designing, implementing, and evaluating instructional ideas.

During the first year, eight teachers from different content areas took released time to work with me in developing the project. These sessions began with a discussion of a theoretical issue and evolved into plans for some specific practices the teachers wanted to investigate within their own classrooms.

The first area investigated, and the one in most drastic need of change, was the persistent practice of assigning students to read without focusing on prior knowledge. Typically the teacher would say, "For tomorrow, I want you to read pages 25-30," without any thought about what students knew or needed to know about the topic before they read. Although the teachers understood on a theoretical level the connection between the background knowledge and reading, they were unsure about specific strategies to ensure its use and remained skeptical about its merits in terms of class time.

Improving a sophomore mathematics class

We began our research by considering the question of setting the stage before students read: Should teachers take the time to elicit and develop appropriate background knowledge before students begin to read? Because we could not assign subjects randomly as one does in a true experiment, we had to modify our procedure. We set up a modified experiment in two sophomore geometry classes taught by one teacher. With this modified procedure, the class that typically did better on chapter tests became the control group and the lower achieving class became the experimental class. If the lower achieving class could perform as well as the control class or better, we could feel confident that a particular learning strategy was effective. The reading materials (a chapter on indirect proofs from the students' geometry text) and time (one class period) were kept constant across conditions.

The teacher assigned the control class to read the chapter and study the sample proofs. The students were free to ask questions during and after reading. Following the reading, the teacher lectured about indirect proofs and did some sample problems. Next, the students did some problems on the board.

For the experimental group, the teacher taught the same lesson, but the emphasis was different in that it required more student participation in reading. Before assigning the reading, she put key vocabulary on the board and had students brainstorm about the meanings of the words. She then wrote a summary of student comments on the board, clarified any misconceptions, and added any needed information. Next, the students listed two or three ideas that they hoped to gain from the selection and read the material silently. Following discussion and rereading, the students practiced doing the sample problems.

Both the experimental and control classes did the problems at the end of the chapter as a test.

As predicted, the instructional procedure applied to the experimental group led to better performance. The experimental geometry students did 31 percent better on the test than did the control group. These data certainly convinced the mathematics teacher of the importance of setting the stage before students read.

To help change the instructional routines of other teachers in the project, I arranged for a "research chat" over lunch, where the math teacher presented her data. Other teachers set up similar experiments in their classrooms and found that results generalized across content areas. Prereading activities started to become standard practice in the content classrooms.

We conducted another experiment in several junior high mathematics classes where we investigated the merits of using writing as an active learning strategy. We used four different classes taught by the same teacher and randomly assigned two classes to the control condition and two to the experimental. We were satisfied that the groups were relatively equivalent in mathematical ability, given that there were no significant differences between our experimental and control class on a mathematics test given the week before the experiment. For three weeks, the instructor had his experimental classes keep a journal of mathematical definitions and practice writing word problems modeled after examples in the text. In addition, students wrote one and two sentence summaries in their journals explaining key mathematical concepts. The same content was covered in the control classes, but the students did not have any writing assignments. At the end of the three week period, both classes did the same computational and word problems as a test. The experimental class did significantly better (9 percent) on the test than the control group.

We summarized the results of this experiment in a newsletter distributed throughout the district. Suddenly writing began to emerge as part of the mathematics curriculum.

Improving language arts

We conducted another series of experiments in ninth grade language arts classes to assess the effect of writing on long term retention of vocabulary. Our ninth grade English teachers used a passive instructional approach to teaching vocabulary. They presented their students with a list of fifteen new words to learn on Monday. Students looked up the definitions in the dictionary and wrote them as a test on Friday. In an effort to modify this instructional routine and generate more student activity, we decided to incorporate writing as part of vocabulary instruction and to evaluate the procedure experimentally. For the first part of the experiment, we used two ninth grade English classes taught by the same teacher. On Monday, we gave each class the same list of fifteen vocabulary words. In the control class, the students looked up three words a day in the dictionary and wrote out their definitions. By Friday they had completed this task with all fifteen words. With the experimental class, the students had the same daily exposure to three words, but instead of writing definitions they combined them into one meaningful sentence. They followed the same procedure for the remainder of the week until they had practiced all fifteen words. Two weeks later, the teacher assigned students to write out the definitions of the words as a test. She had actually biased the test favoring the control group since the criterion measure was identical to the strategy the students had used for learning the words. Nevertheless, the experimental students did 43 percent better on the test.

While these results were intriguing, the teacher still was not convinced. Perhaps the experimental class was simply a better class. She decided to redo the experiment, but switch conditions, making the previous experimental class the control and vice versa. Practically the same results occurred on the long term test where the students wrote out definitions of the words. The experimental class did 30 percent better on the test than did the control class.

Armed with this replication, the English teacher began to convert the other teachers to the merits of having students use vocabulary words in their own writing. According to her data, writing was an active learning strategy that helped students integrate new words into their own working vocabulary. Learning dictionary definitions was not as effective for building background knowledge in vocabulary.

Improving history instruction

We did another series of experiments to help teachers understand how to use learning guides for active learning and self-monitoring. We developed a notetaking procedure that we dubbed the Montana Plan. It is not new except, perhaps, the form of delivery.

The format is simple. Students divide their paper lengthwise into two columns. In the left column they include key words or questions describing an essential concept or main idea presented in the reading selection. In the right column they record information elaborating on the main points. Upon completing their notes, they use them as a study guide by covering the information on the right and then testing themselves using the information in the left column.

Since the prerequisite for the guide is an understanding of how to extract main ideas from content selections, teachers spend considerable class time teaching students how to develop their guides. At first they are directive to the point of modeling for the students how to read for main ideas and to convert the main points to questions on the guide. Several teachers found it helpful to begin by giving their students sample guides, gradually making the examples less complete until students were writing their own guides.

Nevertheless, several instructional problems arose, which we were able to address successfully through classroom research. While the goal is to teach students to create their own two column notes, several teachers persisted in supplying their students with teacher made guides. Apparently they feared their students would miss something if they were allowed to construct their own guides, but the teacher guides were a crutch contributing to continued student dependence and passivity. Again, the sensitive approach to the problem was to involve the teachers in an experiment.

We used two American history classes taught by the same teacher; both classes had received similar exposure to learning guides. In one class, the teacher distributed a learning guide he had written over one chapter. In the other class, he instructed students to create their own guides over the selection. The experimental class again was the one performing less well on the previous test. A week later, the students took a test over the chapter. As predicted, the experimental group performed significantly better on the test (18 percent) than the control class. Because of these data, teachers began changing their instructional strategies by having students construct their own guides.

Another experiment involving learning guides adds further credence to the importance of student activity and self-monitoring strategies. One history teacher expressed concern that his students were not using the guide adequately for self-testing. To convince his students of the importance of such activity, he conducted a one week experiment. In the experimental class, he instructed his students to use the last five minutes of class to study from their learning guides. He gave explicit directions to cover the right portion of the guide and use the key words and questions on the left to test themselves over the material. In the other class, he told his students to study without any specific direction to use the study guides. The control class had their two column notes available, but most chose not to use them for studying. On the test given at the end of the week, the experimental students did much better on this test than the control class (21 percent). The teacher then shared these data with his students. As a result, more students began to use their guides for self-monitoring of performance. (It is interesting to note that this teacher is using the experimental approach to convince students, much as I have used it to convince teachers.)

By our third year, we decided to conduct a more extensive experiment. Our purpose was twofold. First, we wanted to provide a somewhat more elegant test of project effectiveness than those described for the development of specific strategies. Second, we wanted to marshal more evidence favoring a content reading and writing approach in hopes of convincing the remainder of our high school staff to participate.

We conducted an experimental control pre/postevaluation with eight junior level American history classes taught by four different teachers. While these teachers had similar professional histories, only two of the four had participated in the project.

During the first week of school all four teachers had their students read and study a four page selection on the 1920s. After students had read and studied the material for forty minutes, using any method they wished, the teachers collected the selections and any notes the students had taken. The next day the students took a free recall test followed by a twenty-five item multiple choice assessment covering the content of the reading selection. Three months later the teachers administered the same test as a posttest. None of the teachers had yet come to the section in their books about the 1920s, so we assumed that the material was of equal familiarity for all students. We felt that if our project was working, students who had been taught how to read and study content material as part of course instruction would show better pre/posttest gains than those who had not received a reading and learning emphasis in their social studies courses. As you can see in Figures 1 and 2, the gains made by our experimental classes are far more impressive than those made by our control classes. The growth is particularly dramatic on the free recall assessment. Such growth is to be expected since we have taught students a variety of studying and learning strategies that should make a difference with both organization and retrieval of information.

After students completed the posttest, we asked them to write a paragraph describing the reading and studying strategies they used with the selection. We found clear differences between the two groups. The most common response made by the control students was that they simply read the selection over a few times. This response varied considerably from those of the experimental students, who responded with a variety of specific strategies such as underlining, summarizing, questioning, and notetaking. In addition, a majority of the experimental students used some type of self-testing strategy to monitor how well they were learning the information. Many actually wrote study questions and practiced answering them, while others tested themselves by mentally recalling information or

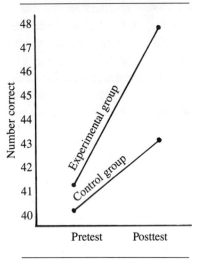

Figure 1
**Growth in experimental
and control social studies
students as measured
by a multiple choice test**

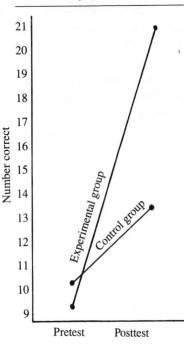

Figure 2
**Growth in experimental
and control social studies
students as measured
by free recall**

by writing summaries or notes from memory. They would then re-read as necessary to learn specific information.

We disseminated the results of our investigation to faculty through newsletters and we also made sure our students were well aware of the experimental results. Classroom based research again played an essential role in changing teaching behavior. The control teachers began to show some interest in project participation.

Thus, a combination of theory and classroom experimentation turned out to be a sensitive and successful way to integrate basic theoretical notions into classroom practice. This combination led to the development of a specific program for teaching reading in the content areas, a program we incorporated throughout our district from grade four through high school. It is interesting to note that the thrust of the project, the development of active student learners, parallels the teachers' active involvement in applying research to their own teaching. The students have a sense of ownership of their own learning, just as teachers have ownership of the project.

Within district dissemination occurred by having teachers train other teachers. We learned that peer training is a particularly effective means of gaining acceptance for curricular change. Teachers' enthusiasm for what they have accomplished kindles the curiosity of their colleagues and makes more of an impression than would a lecture by an outside expert. Project teachers continue to teach graduate courses in content reading, give conference talks, and conduct district sponsored workshops.

Throughout this entire developmental process, our goal was to create a project based on teacher participation and suggestion. Nothing was ever imposed. There was never an administrative dictum—we let the ripples spread as they may. We realize we will never reach everyone. There always will be those who resist change or who have calcified and prefer not to deviate from their entrenchment. Yet, most teachers have participated, and we can now say that all students who graduate from our high school have learned how to learn with a variety of methods from a variety of teachers.

A blueprint for improving achievement in the content areas

In the past two years, we have been supported by the National Diffusion Network to disseminate our content reading program and our method of curricular change to various school districts throughout the country. Typically, this involves a three day workshop presented by content teachers from Kalispell. We have found that having content teachers train other content teachers has considerable ecological validity for workshop participants.

The inservice and corresponding manuals we have developed in science, social studies, and language arts cover the same topics for all teachers, but we have developed different model instructional materials and examples for the three subject areas. We start by discussing teacher assessment of textbooks and students and then move on to main idea development, learning strategies, vocabulary, and directed reading activity – four topics that describe instructional strategies for implementation.

We begin our workshops with a brief overview of the project's history and a discussion of the theoretical components outlined previously in this chapter. We then introduce the practical instructional components.

Text assessment. In this component, participating teachers learn how to analyze the reading level, content, and organization of their texts. Participants evaluate their own texts using an assessment checklist. We then present some specific strategies for helping students use text organization as an aid to comprehension.

Student assessment. Participants learn how to write informal tests over their texts, such as content informal reading inventories, to evaluate whether students can read effectively the texts used in their own classes. We provide time in the workshop for teachers to begin developing these informal evaluations.

Main idea development. Participants learn how the organization of text influences its comprehensibility and how to help students familiarize themselves with the author's style of main idea development. They also learn active procedures (summarizing, underlining, notetaking) for extracting main ideas from text and strategies for teaching students to self-monitor their progress in understanding main ideas. They then create a plan for teaching their students some of their own main idea strategies and discuss procedures for evaluating their ideas experimentally.

Learning strategies. For the teacher participants, we model a variety of procedures designed to help students organize material for understanding and retaining information. They learn to organize verbal and written information into two and three column notetaking formats, to organize information through various charting procedures, and to monitor their learning through self-questioning and discussion. In addition, we introduce teachers to memory development and test taking strategies. Teachers practice categorization and clustering techniques they can use with their students for reducing the number of key ideas remembered. Participants also learn procedures for helping students organize information for essay tests. We then allow time for the teachers to adapt ideas within their own texts.

Vocabulary. We introduce teachers to specific strategies such as the use of context, structural analysis, and categorization. In addition, we stress a variety of writing assignments for incorporating vocabulary into students' working vocabulary.

Directed Reading Activity. We demonstrate to participants an example Directed Reading Activity (DRA), since it incorporates everything we have presented in the workshop into an overall approach to teaching reading in the content areas. We broadly define DRA's as activities teachers and students use before, during, and after reading to generate comprehension and retention. After modeling a DRA, we have workshop participants create one over a selection they are about to assign to their own students. We tell them that the DRA must include procedures for eliciting and developing background knowledge and direct instruction in vocabulary, main idea, and learning strategies.

Throughout our workshop presentation, we present specific strategies using an instructional procedure that we recommend for all content reading and writing instruction. Our instruction is direct and includes four sequential steps: introduction, teacher modeling, guided practice, and independent application. The following example demonstrates how these four components can be used in the classroom to teach students how to understand main ideas through text organization.

1. *Introduction.* The instructor first develops rules or steps for analyzing the organization of a text. The teacher and students discuss the various ways main ideas can be presented and identify specific procedures for discerning the author's style. For example, a text may be written with main ideas noted in the introductory paragraph or the opening sentences of each paragraph. Through discussion, the instructor helps students realize that understanding an author's style is a prerequisite to comprehension.

2. *Teacher modeling.* Direct instruction continues by teacher modeling. The teacher "talks through" or verbally models his/her own reading of a section of the students' text. During this verbal monologue, students hear and observe how their teacher employs text organization to comprehend meaning. With such modeling, students learn the why, when, where, and how of each new strategy.

3. *Guided practice.* Next, students attempt to use the modeled strategies while reading on their own. Class time is allowed for discussing how text organization helped (or hindered) student comprehension. We stress the importance of rereading in cases where text organization is not immediately obvious. Students discuss concepts presented in the text and authors' use of specific structural patterns, such as problem solution or comparison and contrast, to develop main points. They also discuss specific contextual signals denoting importance, such as "The main point here is," "In summary," or "As a result."

4. *Independent application.* After sufficient guided practice, students apply independently what they have learned about text structure for comprehension. Even at this independent stage, class time is set aside for discussion, particularly when students are confronted with poorly written material or material containing many unfamiliar concepts.

Validation. Throughout the workshop we also talk about setting up classroom research studies to validate ideas we have presented as well as participants' instructional innovations. We recommend using procedures similar to those used in our own project development.

At the conclusion of the workshop, teachers will have evaluated their texts; developed a preliminary student assessment; and developed learning activities incorporating learning guides, vocabulary instruction, and directed reading activities within their own course areas. Because teachers are provided opportunities for such application, they leave our sessions with strategies they can implement in their classrooms. Moreover, they also leave with a four stage instructional procedure for teaching and an understanding of how to use action research for involving themselves, their students, and their colleagues in developing and evaluating learning strategies.

The teachers and administrators who attend our workshop are responsible for disseminating the project throughout their own district. Their first task is to try some of the ideas within their own classes and to set up some classroom experiments to evaluate effectiveness in terms of student performance. We recommend that administrators adopt a class and get their feet wet along with the teachers. In addition, administrators need to take responsibility for finding time for teachers to brag about their successes. After about three months, the teachers and administrators should begin making plans for disseminating the project to other staff.

We have developed a specific program that spreads across the curriculum and ultimately produces better learners. We have evolved an effective method for inducing change in a school system. The key ingredient to change is gaining teacher acceptance and involvement by first providing teachers with a theoretical structure and statement of the problem. Next, we show teachers how to apply theory in their own situations by involving them in developing materials and evaluating methods. This approach creates a strong identification so teachers feel they have actively developed an effective teaching method. Such identification assumes continued use and development of a program. Finally, our method of developing an active, creative teacher parallels the method of learning we have developed for our students. We develop theoretical background information and then make teachers active participants in the program.

One of the important contributions of our project is that it stimulates students, teachers, and administrators to think critically about the learning process. Such thought and effort is bound to be rewarding.

References

Anderson, T.H., and Armbruster, B. Reader and text: Studying strategies. In W. Otto and S. White (Eds.), *Reading expository material.* New York: Academic Press, 1982, 219-239.
Andre, M.E.D.A., and Anderson, T.H. The development and evaluation of a self-questioning study technique. *Reading Research Quarterly,* 1979, *14,* 605-623.

Armbruster, B.B., and Anderson, T.H. *Content area textbooks.* Urbana, IL: University of Illinois, Center for the Study of Reading, 1981.

Baker, L. Comprehension monitoring: Identifying and coping with text confusions. *Journal of Reading Behavior,* 1980, *11,* 365-374.

Baker, L., and Stein, N. The development of prose comprehension skills. In C. Santa and B. Hayes (Eds.), *Children's prose comprehension: Research and practice.* Newark, DE: International Reading Association, 1981, 7-43.

Brown, A. Learning how to learn from reading. In J. Langer and M.T. Smith-Burke (Eds.), *Reader meets author/Bridging the gap.* Newark, DE: International Reading Association, 1983, 26-54.

Dooling, J., and Lachman, R. Effects of comprehension on retention of prose. *Journal of Experimental Psychology,* 1971, *88,* 216-222.

Gates, Arthur. Recitation as a factor in memorizing. *Archives of Psychology,* 1917, *40.*

Ross, S. Oral summary as a review strategy for enhancing recall of textual material. *Journal of Educational Psychology,* 1976, *68,* 689-695.

Santa, C., Abrahms, L., and Santa, J. The effect of notetaking on the recognition and recall of information. *Journal of Reading Behavior,* 1979, *11,* 249-260.

Schallert, D.L. The significance of knowledge: A synthesis of research related to schema theory. In W. Otto and S. White (Eds.), *Reading expository material.* New York: Academic Press, 1982, 13-48.

Stotsky, S. Research on reading and writing relationship: A synthesis and suggested direction. *Language Arts,* 1983, *60,* 627-642.

Prelude

A t about the same time Carol Santa began her efforts in Kalispell, a team from the University of Illinois and Illinois State University led by Robert Tierney and David Tucker also began using and studying the teacher as researcher model while working with volunteer teachers at Metcalf Laboratory School on the ISU campus. Over a period of several years, what has evolved at Metcalf is a true teacher-researcher collaboration in the best sense of that term. The participants in this collaborative effort have managed to develop a program that, as of this writing, has permitted teachers to take full control of their own learning and research activities. This chapter has as much of a message for university staff as it does for teachers. It reminds us that university experts should not take all the responsibility for planning and presenting staff development sessions. The approach in this chapter is very much in the mutual adaptation tradition; it is grass roots continuing education in its most basic form.

Robert J. Tierney
David L. Tucker
Margaret C. Gallagher
Avon Crismore
P. David Pearson

10

The Metcalf Project: A teacher-researcher collaboration

T he word *remote* might be used to describe the usual relationship between researchers and teachers, between theory and practice, and between teaching and learning. Researchers seem content to suggest principles of effective teaching, espouse new methods, or delineate the implications of theory for teaching and learning, while remaining separate from the everyday forces in operation in real classrooms. Researchers seem to prefer advising teachers from a distance. Teachers tend to display similar predilections. They seem content to keep researchers at bay and sometimes even maintain a distance between themselves and their own students. For example, teachers are likely to expend their energies negotiating with a set of curriculum objectives in a teacher's guide rather than refining their student watching skills or adjusting their instruction to meet the idiosyncratic needs of students.

The Metcalf Project was initiated to explore a different type of relationship; to unite disparate factions involved in teaching reading and writing; and to establish a collaboration between theory and practice, between teaching and learning, and between researchers and teachers.

The Metcalf Project originated in Spring 1982 with a series of discussions among staff at the Center for the Study of Reading at the University of Illinois at Urbana-Champaign (CSR), Illinois State University (ISU), and the Metcalf Laboratory School at ISU. David Tucker at ISU expressed interest in developing with CSR a working relationship that would complement his role in staff and curriculum development at the Metcalf Laboratory School. He suggested that the CSR staff might use Metcalf as a site for applying some of their recent research findings. Metcalf staff members were interested in becoming more actively involved with the research community, in keeping with Metcalf's mission as a laboratory school.

The prospect of developing a working relationship with the Metcalf-ISU staff was appealing to the CSR staff. We were interested in working in a situation where there might be give and take between teachers and researchers. Rather than asking teachers to implement certain practices or taking over their classrooms to conduct a laboratory like instructional study, we wanted Metcalf to be a site for a project on teacher change based on teacher-researcher collaboration.

We decided to invite teachers to explore reading comprehension and composition in their classrooms in a manner that supported teacher decision making and initiative. Reseachers would share ideas, but instead of mandating change, they would help teachers observe what they were doing, consider alternatives, and examine the potential of changes in practice. Teachers would develop an instructional repertoire based on assessment of the effectiveness of different instructional practices; moreover, they would develop an appreciation for teaching and learning.

In other words, we wanted to establish a partnership between researchers and practitioners. Teachers would make decisions based on what they had gleaned from observations of their teaching and from their discussions with researchers. Researchers would expose teachers to new theory and research in reading comprehension and writing, but were expected to avoid offering direct advice. Their role was to help support and refine teacher decision making. The logical extension of this support role was the expectation that eventually the researchers would be displaced by the teachers. As teachers became better problem solvers, they would generate their own momentum for change and would, in turn, become support personnel for other teachers.

A description of the Metcalf Project

Since its inception, the Metcalf Project's goals have not changed, but its form has. From year to year, the project has pursued different activities to meet the changing needs and expanding skills of the teachers. The first year, teachers reviewed and reacted to new ideas and adopted variations of them in their classrooms. The project was restricted to teachers and students in grades four, five, and six who volunteered to participate in the project. By the end of the second year, teachers had explored several projects, developed particular interests, cultivated attitudes of genuine curiosity, and acquired considerable independence. In the third year, the project expanded to include volunteer teachers at other grade levels. Throughout this time, the advisory team included four CSR staff members, the school principal, the director of the laboratory schools at ISU, and staff from ISU's college of education. What follows is a more detailed description of activities pursued each year.

Year one

The first semester was used for planning. While we had defined the goals of the project, we had not determined how they might be achieved. Our first problems were to specify a process for change and to define the framework within which change could occur.

We wanted teachers to ask themselves what they wanted to teach, how they wanted to teach, and how they might judge their own effectiveness. This meant teachers had to develop the confidence, willingness, and knowledge to explore and evaluate pedagogical alternatives. To describe this view of teaching, we began to use the phrase "teaching as a continuing experiment."

In Fall 1982, we invited all six teachers of grades four, five, and six to participate in the project. We described our plan and stressed that, while we would be discussing specific instructional strategies in reading and writing, our goal was not to have teachers adopt these strategies, replacing current ones. Rather, we hoped to explore how teachers examine pedagogical alternatives. They themselves, their thinking, and their practice would be under observation. Specifically, the observation would involve interviews, questionnaires, and videotaping of ongoing instruction at regular intervals.

Rich Schuler, director of the laboratory schools and acting principal of Metcalf School, relieved participating teachers of some of their routine committee work and provided a substitute teacher so teachers could meet with project staff during the school day. Five of the six teachers agreed to participate in the project.

The project began formally in January 1983. For two weeks we conducted interviews with teachers, administered questionnaires, and made videotapes of one reading lesson and one content area lesson (science or social studies) for each teacher. After two weeks of collecting baseline data, we embarked on the project proper.

Each month for a period of three months the group (teachers and ISU and CSR staff) studied one of three topics: background knowledge, reading-writing relationships, and the role of discussion in reading classrooms. These three topics were chosen for a number of reasons. Background knowledge was selected since it is an area for which there is a great deal of research support and obvious classroom applications. Reading-writing relationships and discussion were identified as important areas despite a dearth of research in these areas. Furthermore, the teachers were obviously interested in both topics.

Each month consisted of the following circle of activities:

Week 1. Researchers presented an overview of the topic.

Week 2. The group considered classroom implications stemming from the overview, readings dealing with the topic, and observations of their videotapes. They generated questions and guidelines (called focus sheets) to help focus their thinking.

Week 3. In advisory sessions, each teacher met with one of the researchers who acted as an advisor. Each teacher decided on a particular question to explore. These meetings were followed by a group meeting during which teachers and advisors shared their plans for a trial run.

Week 4. In advisory sessions, we reviewed what had happened during the trial run and discussed adjustments or modifications to the original plan. Brief meetings of the entire group allowed teacher/advisor pairs to present their progress to date.

At the completion of the cycle for each topic, the entire group convened to share reactions, observations, and preliminary findings and to identify unresolved issues and new questions. Each advisor/teacher team wrote a summary report of its project, then new teams formed for a new topic.

To illustrate more fully what teachers did during this initial phase, we include some examples of the material developed. Figure 1 contains focus sheets listing the guidelines generated by the group in response to our presentation on background knowledge. Figure 2 contains guidelines for reading-writing relationships.

Figure 1
Focus sheets for background knowledge

Topic: Background knowledge

1. Researching what students know

- Pick out key words in a selection. Discuss with students how these might be related to something familiar that students may have read about or seen.
- Look at pictures. Based on the pictures, make predictions about the characters or the story.
- Draw out experiences students may have had that would be relevant to the topic.
- Use maps to learn more about a location specified in the selection.
- Suggest or have available supplementary reading on related topics.
- Select some key words; ask students to free associate; record responses on board.
- Discuss with students a concept or situation you feel will be analogous (for them) to the one they will be reading about.
- Have some students serve as experts on particular topics.
- Simulate some part of the experience in the selection in the classroom. This will give students some first hand experience.
- Preread a selected passage; have students predict what will be forthcoming.

  In all of the above activities, the teacher must:
- Analyze the knowledge domain required. What does the child need to know and think about in order to understand?

Figure 1
Focus sheets for background knowledge (continued)

- Introduce child centered rather than teacher or text centered knowledge.
- Provide more than a definitional experience for children. The teacher should be concerned with relational ties between old and new information.

2. Mobilizing what students know

- Ask, "Have you ever felt that way?" Invite students to identify with characters.
- Predict how the story will end; ask students what makes them think so.
- Ask the same question three or four times; if students change their answers, ask them why.
- Have students generate questions.
- Ask students to adopt a point of view about something in the story. Ask one student to adopt one point of view and another the opposite point of view.
- Have students take a position about what they have read; ask them to justify it.
- Ask students what they know about a topic.
- Ask students to recollect something you consider relevant and that you are sure they know.
- Get students to visualize something by drawing a quick sketch.
- Ask students to make comparisons—to draw analogies between the new information they are encountering and old, more familiar information (e.g., Canada and U.S., states and provinces).
- Display information in chart form.
- Encourage students to become engaged with the text by asking them to read knowing they later will be asked to perform a skit or initiate a character or story activity.
- Have students dramatize parts of a selection; ask them to act as tour guides.

3. Seeing what students know and helping them watch their knowledge grow and change

- Help children see how the pieces fit together and form a whole.
- Encourage children to bring to school information they consider relevant (maps, books).
- After students have free associated, organize that information on the board or on an overhead projector.
- Have students compare what they already know (prereading knowledge) with the information they have gained from reading their text (perhaps by filling in empty slots on a chart).
- Ask experts in class to prepare a test. Ask others to help evaluate the aptness of the questions for the text read.

Figure 2
Focus sheets for reading-writing relationships

Checklists for providing reading and writing opportunities

Are students being given opportunities for full writing and reading experiences?

Planning
- In writing, are you providing time for self-initiated planning?
- In reading, are you providing for self-initiated planning?
- In writing, are you encouraging students to immerse themselves in the characters and events they describe? (first person, third person, using dialogue, vivid descriptions)

Aligning
- In reading, are you encouraging students to immerse themselves in characters and events?
- In writing, are you providing opportunities to talk through ideas? Do rough drafts? Override concern for low level problems? Experiences?

Drafting
- In reading, are you providing opportunities to reread? Jot down ideas? Override low level problems?
- In writing, are students encouraged to share what they have written? To talk about what they are trying to do? How well?

Revise/
Conference
- In writing, are students encouraged to revise, edit, and publish?
- In reading, are students encouraged to share what they have read? Their goals? How well?
- In reading, are students encouraged to revise and edit?

Are you providing students with writing opportunities during reading?

Do you give opportunities for writing
- Prior to reading?
- During reading?
- After reading?

Are you discussing how writers use what they learn from their reading in their writing? Followup?

Are you providing students with reading opportunities during writing?

Do you give opportunities for reading
- Prior to writing (e.g., for researching ideas, learning about techniques)?
- After drafts (e.g., checking for accuracy, richness, techniques, impact)?
- Self-checking en route to revision?
- For purposes of editing?

Are you discussing how readers might use what they learn from their writing in their reading?

Figure 2
Focus sheets for reading-writing relationships (continued)

Are you providing students with opportunities to talk about how they read and write and to hear other people (including yourself) talk about how they read and write?

Are you encouraging students to have full and independent reading and writing experiences?

Helping students plan for writing

Planning involves providing opportunities to

Research	• Brainstorm • Add facts, bearing in mind genre and context • Organize ideas • Tap other sources (reference material, books, interviews) • Explore senses
Adopt a stance or purpose	• Narrow or broad focus. What is my main point? (Who? What? Why?) What is the significance?
Arrange	• Choose storyteller • Order events, ideas • Highlight, set priorities
Anticipate effects	• Scare, amuse, suspend my reader • Learn outcomes
Share plans	• Discuss with peer or teacher (intentions)

Checklist for planning

Are students
    ___ brainstorming?
    ___ generating ideas for all the slots (who, what, where, why)?
    ___ adding facts based on context (audience, publication)?
    ___ tapping different resources (books, people)?
    ___ exploring what they know about a topic through all their senses?
    ___ clustering ideas?
    ___ deciding what ideas are most important?
    ___ thinking about the focus (broad, narrow)?
    ___ considering order?
    ___ considering storyteller?
    ___ considering formalness?
    ___ considering devices?
    ___ considering effect on reader's thinking and senses?
    ___ considering what they are trying to say?
    ___ sharing plans?
    ___ revising plans?

                          Tierney, Tucker, Gallagher, Crismore, Pearson

Figure 2
Focus sheets for reading-writing relationships (continued)

A tentative agenda

Day one	• Writing experiences with no planning
Day two	• Writing experiences with planning (10 to 15 minutes)
Day three	• Generic plan for planning (checklist emerges with class discovery or teachers discuss given plan) • Writing experience with planning
Day four	• Discuss planning

Throughout the semester, teachers generated the equivalent of fifteen miniresearch projects ranging from the effects of different modes of discussion on pupil involvement and the quality of their arguments to the effects of visualization experiences on the reading of selected students in the low reading group. To present a clearer picture of these minitryouts, we describe in detail two projects initiated in fourth grade classrooms.

A study of background knowledge

Charlene Behrends decided to focus on the topic of background knowledge. After analyzing a videotape of her teaching, she questioned whether she was introducing so many concepts prior to reading a selection that the concepts were treated superficially. The students did not seem to be absorbed in what they read, and were not able to proceed independently. Behrends set two objectives for herself. First, to get the students more involved with text selections and topics, she would help them use their own ideas to complete a map of their prior knowledge of a topic. Second, to integrate old and new information, she would provide directives and questions to ensure that students would relate what they knew about the topic to the selection itself. Furthermore, rather than deal with so many concepts, she would select a few and tie them together.

The second week, an excerpt about loneliness from *Charlotte's Web* was the story in the basal reader. Behrends led the reading group in a discussion of loneliness, asking students to predict what the story could be about. Then she worked with the children to develop a list of animals on a farm, telling how as pets they would be different from farm animals. This led to a discussion of how pets might feel lonely and how friendship combats loneliness. In analyzing the tape of the second lesson, Behrends noted that the lesson appeared to tie together better, the children were more absorbed in it, and they seemed better able to read independently.

Behrends kept two questions in mind as she presented and evaluated further lessons. Am I giving students chances to research what they know about a topic? How am I helping students assume the role of expert?

Behrends completed the last two weeks by transferring what she had learned about the role of background knowledge to lessons in other reading groups and also to social studies. As a result of the month's work, two main changes occurred in her teaching. She developed the expert notion by having students generate lists of what they knew about a topic before they read. Second, she dealt with fewer concepts, but dealt with them in greater depth.

A study of revision and planning

Wanda Bradford was in her first year of teaching and had been assigned to a fourth grade self-contained classroom. Prior to our discussion of reading-writing relationships, her students did very little writing. In fact, she doubted whether the students were capable of doing much writing. With this in mind, she approached the topic of reading-writing relationships with two questions. To what extent were students capable of generating extended written responses to a topic they were reading in social studies? What influence might planning have on student writing? The first question stemmed from our discussion of reading-writing relationships and her assumption that students lacked the skills needed to write. The second question was an extension of her interest in the role of planning and background knowledge. She did the following things to explore these two questions.

1. After students read and discussed a section in the social studies text, Bradford asked them to portray and to interview characters in the chapter. Half the class was in-

structed to conduct an interview and to portray a character without any previous planning. The other half was allowed time to plan their interview questions and read about the character they were to portray. While Group 1 members were interviewing one another, Group 2 members were planning and preparing their interviews.

2. The next day, students in Group 1, who had not used pre-planning, were asked to write their interviews in story form. Students in Group 2, who planned for their interviews, proceeded to interview one another. Then the class discussed briefly the differences between the groups and generated a list of advantages to planning.

3. On the third day, Group 1 students revised their summaries. Group 2 wrote about their interviews. Both groups were told to make their summaries as interesting as they could.

4. The entire class was divided into four groups on the basis of the person they had interviewed. In the groups, students presented their summaries to one another and selected a representative to summarize for the whole class. The whole class presentation was conducted as if the people were being interviewed on television. After these presentations, the students discussed the interviews and how planning contributed to their interviews.

Bradford's project answered some questions and suggested others. First, she discovered that she had underestimated her students' capabilities as writers. Second, she found that writing was useful for extending reading activities and for followup reading of social studies material. Third, she and her pupils recognized that planning contributed significantly to how efficient and successful students were as writers and interviewers. An independent rating of the stories suggested that essays produced by students who planned were better, when judged holistically, than those produced by other students. A fourth finding took Bradford by surprise: The revisions were not an improvement over the first drafts. She explored this issue in year two.

By June 1983 we could see changes. Teachers and researchers were asking more questions about reading, writing, teaching, learning, and change than when we began the project. In terms of our goals, we felt the teachers were becoming objective observers of their own teaching. Furthermore, instructional initiatives teachers had explored crept into their teaching at other times.

For the university team, the process of working collaboratively with teachers to help them think about instructional problems and goals was radically different from the usual experience of delivering a prepackaged set of instructions for implementing procedures. Just as the teachers' practices were being subjected to close scrutiny and change, so too were many of our ideas about change, effective instructional procedures, and ways to communicate those ideas.

Year two

At the close of the school year, the administration of Metcalf School changed. The new director, Dennis Kelly, continued to extend support to the project, as did Al Jurenas, the new principal.

Year two preparations began in the summer. For three days the project group met to evaluate the first year of the project and to plan for the second. Decisions ranged from what topics should be the focus of year two to the suggestion of changes in the organizational framework for achieving the goals of the project.

An important feature of this meeting was the sense of community that had developed during the first year. This was heralded by what may seem a trivial development. The teachers chose to change the title of the researchers from advisors to partners. As year two began, we knew teachers had to become integrally involved as decision makers in all aspects of the project. If this project was to endure after the researchers left, teacher control had to be established. During year one, we felt as if most decisions were being made by the researchers. Indeed, there was a tendency for the teachers to expect us to make decisions for them. In year two, everybody in the project was involved in making decisions.

In year one we explored three topic areas and changed the teacher/researcher pairing for each topic; in year two, each teacher chose to explore a single topic in depth. In addition, each teacher worked with the same partner (or rather the same team) for the entire year and did not receive released time.

Consistent with the goals of the project, we adopted a problem solving framework that we used for all projects in year two. This involved five steps.

1. *Selecting a general area of interest.* Each teacher chose a general area on which to concentrate during the year. Given the common interests of the teachers, we formed two subgroups: background knowledge and discussion and reading-writing relationships. Within each subgroup there were pairs of teacher/researcher collaborators.

2. *Defining the problem.* Teachers were expected to observe their own teaching and their students' performance and to think about what goals might be set. At the same time, researchers provided some input on the topic. Using this input, teachers and partners defined the focus of the projects and shared objectives with their respective subgroups.

3. *Securing baseline data and planning projects.* Team members collected some baseline information and discussed the students' abilities. We analyzed videotapes and we examined students' responses to checklists, tests, and day to day teaching. This cycle of planning and gathering data was repeated throughout the project.

4. *Implementing the project and securing feedback on progress.* Feedback and revision were integral parts of implementation. Plans were revised as the need for changes became evident. On a weekly basis, teachers and partners (or the entire team) discussed what had occurred, viewed videotapes, and discussed implementation. Throughout the project, teachers and partners examined developments, noted improvements in student performance, and discussed other signs of progress.

5. *Sharing the project*. Periodically, teachers and partners shared their projects with their topic team or with the entire project group. This provided additional opportunities for revision. At the end of the project, each teacher/partner pair prepared a written report of what had transpired.

Two teachers selected discussion as their general area of interest. This interest stemmed from a desire to explore some of the issues touched on in the previous year. One teacher explored explicit standards and strategies for discussion; another chose to explore how discussions of background knowledge influenced comprehension and learning in social studies. Three teachers had developed an interest in reading-writing relationships and were concerned about their students' weaknesses in revision and critical reading of their own written work. One teacher examined whether instruction in sentence and paragraph structure transfers to informative reading and writing. The other two teachers pursued reading-writing relationships in conjunction with trying to improve their students' critical reading abilities and revision strategies.

Helping students learn to revise

Mary Kay Fairfield, a fifth grade teacher, focused on reading-writing relationships — in particular, how she might integrate these to help her students learn to revise. Some baseline data collected in October suggested that students had a limited sense of revision. To them, revision involved correcting spelling and tidying pages.

As Fairfield and her partner discussed this problem, certain principles and objectives emerged to guide planning for a project. For example, they determined that it was important for students to understand what revision involved and how to revise. They reasoned that if students could distance themselves from their own work, they would be capable of effective revision. Fairfield speculated that peers might help achieve this distance by reading aloud one another's work and providing advice. With these tenets in mind, she developed the following plan:

1. Students discussed the revisions E.B. White made when he wrote *Charlotte's Web*.
2. Students wrote on a topic assigned by the teacher.
3. Students brainstormed about what was involved in revision in order to define the steps involved, then discussed reasons for doing revision.
4. As a group, students examined and discussed possible revision of written work the teacher had saved from previous years.
5. Each student was assigned a peer for input. The peer's job was to offer suggestions to the student for revisions of the composition and to read the composition aloud so the writer could hear it from a distance.

Fairfield encountered several surprises. She had been uncertain of how students would react to discussing E.B. White's revisions and the topic of revision in general, but they loved it. Not only did all the students become actively involved, they shared ideas reflecting their knowledge of the difference between revision (of ideas) and editing (for style and mechanics), and they even demonstrated some feeling for how and when each might be pursued.

However, while the children could talk about revision, they had difficulty actually changing their own work, even with the support of their peers. Students were reluctant to change their texts, and peers tended to offer general praise rather than specific criticisms or suggestions. Fairfield and her research partner (indeed the entire research team) were forced to reexamine their own thinking about revision and to modify the project plan.

Over the next three months, Fairfield continued to work with revision, and she began to see changes. Not only did students begin to revise; their writing in general began to improve. So, too, did their interactions with their peers. And she noticed some carryover to students' reading comprehension. At the end of the year, Fairfield and her partner wrote an article about teaching revision. To appreciate her problem solving initiative, you should be aware that in year one Fairfield had preferred that the researchers tell her what to do. During year two, she assumed the role of initiator and scientist.

The concept of story

Rita Fisher, a sixth grade teacher, was interested in developing her students' understanding of how authors write and revise stories. She had noted that students had limited revision strategies. Her students had no sense of what changes to make, and they tended to have difficulty focusing their attention on specific problem areas. Fisher initiated the following plan.

1. Students discussed key elements that make up a story and how the quality of these features distinguish good stories from mediocre ones.
2. Students created a checklist to apply to a story they had read and to their own stories.
3. Students selected one story feature they felt needed improvement and grouped themselves with other students who were planning to focus on the same feature. The students read several published stories and discussed how those authors developed the feature in question.
4. Students then applied these criteria to one of their own stories and then revised it, paying particular attention to that same feature.

Fisher's hypotheses about the importance of focusing attention and having opinions were confirmed. Students became authorities on how they might improve certain features of their stories and revised their stories accordingly. Furthermore, there was considerable carryover to reading. Students began to read other stories with an eye to how writers craft stories.

Discussion and reading comprehension

Mary Rozum, a fifth grade teacher, was interested in a followup of some of her work in discussion. She was particularly interested in whether students' awareness of the purposes of discussion could influence their subsequent reading comprehension. She designed a project with two specific questions in mind: Will the introduction of activities designed to help students realize the value of discussion result in changes in their perceptions of the role of discussion in learning? If so, will there be any change in the degree of their understanding of the texts they read?

Before introducing the planned activities, Rozum developed and administered a questionnaire designed to assess students' current attitudes toward discussion. After completing the questionnaire, the students held an open discussion about the value of discussion, generating a list of ways discussion contributes to learning.

Working in groups, students developed checklists for how to read and discuss a story and steps for reading and discussing an expository selection. Later, students used these guidelines when discussing their assigned reading.

Rozum readministered the questionnaire to determine whether there were any changes in students' attitudes. She found that students tended to be more positive about the value of discussion. She assessed students' independent reading comprehension through short answer tests on two selected passages. Rozum found that she could document growth in her students' comprehension as well as an improvement in their attitudes toward learning activities.

There were other developments in year two. The most time consuming was the introduction of systematic procedures for monitoring changes in student performance. Project staff members agreed that the commercially available standardized tests being used at Metcalf were inadequate for what we wanted to measure. To collect data that matched the goals of the project, we selected several instruments from scales developed by members of the project staff for use in other studies. Other measures were developed solely for use in the Metcalf Project. At the beginning and end of year two, students involved in the project were administered the following tests:

1. *Reading comprehension assessment.* Three passages were selected for students to respond to: a story from a basal, a social studies selection from a content area text, and a science selection from an encyclopedia. Students read each selection, then wrote a summary, selected questions from a list they deemed most important, and wrote responses to a prepared set of questions.
2. *Writing assessment.* Students were asked to write three compositions and then to revise them. The three writing

prompts were "If I could be anything I wanted to be...," "Describe the Bloomington-Normal area to someone who has never been here," and "Write a story about anything you want to write about."

3. *Attitude measures.* Students responded to parallel reading and writing measures.

4. *Behavioral questionnaires.* Students responded to parallel questionnaires probing reading and writing behaviors students use when reading and writing different texts.

These tests allowed us to monitor student progress systematically, and we also monitored teacher change. Attitudinal changes, teacher initiative, and changes in theoretical perspectives were monitored by transcripts of structured teacher interviews conducted at the beginning and end of each year and notes and transcripts of individual and group meetings held at different times during the course of the project. Changes in the frequency of input from the different parties involved in the project and the nature of comments, complaints, observations, and problem solving tendencies were some of the variables monitored.

Behavioral changes or instructional practices were monitored with the aid of our notes, teacher self-reports, and detailed analyses of videotapes. Beginning in year one, teachers were videotaped on a regular basis twice every week during one reading and one content area lesson. During year two, videotaping occurred less frequently but was systematic in terms of a reading lesson and a content area lesson. Videotapes enabled us to analyze how teacher-student interactions changed during the course of the project and in specific projects.

Year three

In year one, teachers were unsure about their reading and writing instruction. They were interested in having "experts" tell them how to teach. Basically, they were interested in prescription. By the end of year two, reading and writing instruction had become a problem solving experience. The alleged experts had become teachers' partners, and together they were students; that is, they were learning what was occurring as well as what might occur in reading and writing classrooms. The teachers had not only become critical consumers of relevant theory and research; they approached teaching as an ongoing experiment. They were more aware of the ramifications of what they were doing, the rationale underlying their choice of activities, and how and why students were responding as they were.

Our goal for year three was to have the teachers become totally self-initiating. By the end of the year, teachers were to be able to dispense with researchers without any loss of the project's momentum. With this as a goal, the project embarked on a new initiative. All teachers involved in the project agreed to serve as research partners to new recruits. The objective was to have the experienced teacher researchers help other teachers become teacher researchers.

In year three, the partners from years one and two continued working together. In addition to exploring new projects, they developed a plan for working with the new recruits.

Their plan extended the project throughout the school and, possibly, to other schools. It provided a way to extend the collaborations between teachers in the school. Based on the thesis that independent learning arises when learning transfers to teaching, teachers involved in the project continued to grow and change. Finally, the plan supported school based initiatives so that teachers and staff could assume responsibility for maintaining the project and for launching other projects.

Some reflections on the project

At a time when there is pessimism about the quality of teachers and teacher education, it is heartening to be involved in a project that confronts the issue of teacher change. We have studied the constraints on teacher growth, pupil learning, and the possible implications of current thinking about reading and writing. We have studied what it takes to implement curriculum change as well as some of the prerequisites of teacher change. This has resulted from voluntary commitment and collaboration, not from administrative mandates for change. We have been given the privilege of sharing teacher decision making. Our problem solving framework guarantees that we don't abuse that privilege.

Neither the project nor our view of change is short term. Change takes time. Although the change continues, we have some products to show for our time at Metcalf. We have developed some guidelines and instructional products for teaching reading comprehension and writing, and some interesting instructional procedures for observing change in student performance and teacher behavior. Teachers have expanded their thinking about reading and writing and have taken advantage of this thinking in their classrooms. They have incorporated into their teaching a variety of strategies they have tried out themselves or adopted from one another's projects. The project has been shared with other schools that are considering similar projects.

More important to the project's goals is what we have learned about change using this model. We believe we have a useful model for nurturing teacher change as well as translating reading and writing research into practice. We have learned that models of change must be sensitive to the fact that change is a human endeavor. Change requires individual effort, problem solving, negotiation, and a willingness to consider alternatives. New ideas were not embraced overnight; they became part of the teachers' thinking and teaching only with effort, problem solving, negotiation, discussion, and grappling with the ideas. Fortunately, the project capitalized on the idiosyncratic learning tendencies of individuals as they achieved ownership of such ideas.

From our perspective, it was wonderful to be in a situation where we could be participant observers of these changes and be part of the problem solving process. We realize that this process of adopting a problem solving attitude was more important than any educational products. Again, the avoidance of prescription was a major force in helping to develop this attitude.

Finally, the success of the project hinges upon communication. Administrators, researchers, and teacher educators are all talking and sharing. Roles may differ on some dimensions, but we are all teachers, all learners, and all problem solvers interested in improving reading and writing in the classroom.

Tierney, Tucker, Gallagher, Crismore, Pearson

Epilogue

When we put this volume together, we did so in the hope that the principles and case studies would provide school personnel with some ideas about what and how to change school reading programs. We believe we have erred on the side of providing more information about the *how* than the *what*; moreover, we are pleased with that error because we believe there is more information available on new directions school reading programs should take than there is on how to go about implementing whatever changes a staff or a district may decide on. (All one has to do to find a wealth of new curricular ideas is to examine the last dozen or so volumes published by the International Reading Association or to peruse any of the last three or four IRA annual convention programs.)

Since we put together the program and worked on editing this volume, there have been some new developments within IRA that convince us the movement toward changing school reading programs continues to gather momentum. For example, at least a dozen of the sessions at each of the 1985, 1986, and 1987 IRA Conventions focused on changing school reading programs. In 1984, a Special Interest Group on Teaching as a Continuing Experiment was formed; it now gives an award annually to an outstanding teacher-researcher and publishes a newsletter on teacher-researcher activities. In short, there is now considerable knowledge and organization for those who wish to initiate change efforts within their own professional contexts.

We hope this volume may serve to motivate and encourage attempts to improve school reading programs. We remind you that change efforts

- Require much time and energy.
- Need strong leadership based more on continued support, sustenance, and trust than on authority.
- Are based more on transaction among equals than direction from those in power.
- Are more effective when those in helping roles work directly with teachers in their own classrooms.
- Require consensus on clearly stated goals.
- Must be based on the best knowledge we can muster.

Whatever the cost, attempts to improve school reading programs are well worth the effort. In the final analysis, we must engage in such efforts. Our children deserve no less.

PDP